30 DAYS TO *Confident*

A 30 Day Confidence Challenge for Female Athletes

Prepare yourself for your best season yet

CHRISTEN SHEFCHUNAS

30 Days to Confident

A 30 Day Confidence Challenge for Female Athletes

Author: Christen Shefchunas

Editor: Michael Nicloy

Associate Editor: Lyda Rose Haerle

Proofreader: Holly Neumann

Cover Design: Nicole Wurtele
Graphic Designer with The CG Sports Company

Interior Layout: Griffin Mill

Author Photo: Michael Stewart

Published by CG Sports Publishing
Head of Publishing: Michael Nicloy
Publishing Coordinator: Holly Neumann
Marketing Coordinator: Rachel Draffen
Director of Marketing for The CG Sports Company

A Division of The CG Sports Company
www.cgsportsco.com

ISBN: 978-1-7359193-3-1

Quantity order requests can be emailed to:
Publishing@cgsportsmanagement.com

Printed in The United States of America

To all the female athletes who rarely get the spotlight,
yet continue to show up and work their asses off every day.

FOREWORD

by Kara Lynn Joyce

While swimming at the national level, I rarely saw female coaches stand shoulder-to-shoulder with male coaches, but on deck, one woman stood out to me, Christen Shefchunas.

As a coach, Christen instilled confidence in her athletes, a confidence that could be seen and felt by everyone around. That kind of coaching—the intangible kind that doesn't happen in the pool or with a stopwatch—wasn't happening everywhere, even though it's no secret that confidence is a key ingredient to a successful athletic career. I know that for myself, a three-time Olympian, it was an important—if not essential—part of my performing at a high level.

I wasn't the only one who noticed Christen's talents and efforts, and before long, Christen was in demand. Whether it was on a college team or with elite athletes ahead of the Rio Olympics, Christen's wisdom started a ripple effect in swimming, one based on qualities outside the pool that could elevate performance in it.

I founded the Lead Sports Summit for female athletes in 2017 and asked Christen to be a keynote speaker at the event. Watching her deliver her message to 75 teenage girls, she transcended past a discussion of times in the pool or what the girls might've considered off-days in training. She spoke about identifying their "what ifs" that might be holding them back. She encouraged them to define their "truths," the things that they could pull themselves back to in moments of fear. She talked about defining success based on their effort, rather than comparing themselves to others.

Standing in that room, all I could think about was how every girl and woman in sports could benefit from such an empowering message, one that Christen delivers in every aspect of her work.

Confidence is an integral part of every athlete's journey and one that most people have little to no help navigating. But Christen's openness and honesty has helped hundreds of women of all ages redefine the role of confidence in their lives, and 30 Days to Confident will help her reach even more women. Whether coaching on deck or as a professional confidence coach, Christen's ability to connect with female athletes is second to none, and 30 Days to Confident lets you in on that connection, too.

This one's for the girls. The girls who might not feel like they're enough. The girls who need a pep talk. The girls who keep showing up. And the girls who want to take it to the next level.

Kara Lynn Joyce is a 3X Olympian,
Founder and CEO of Lead Sports Co.

INTRODUCTION

My name is Christen Shefchunas, and I come from the swimming world.

I started swimming competitively when I was 12, and I fell in love with it immediately.

When it came time for college, I decided to walk on at the University of Tennessee. My times were not at the Division I level, but I believed that if I surrounded myself with elite athletes and worked my ass off in a great training program, I could be great, too.

I did work my ass off, and I walked out four years later as a four-time All-American. I was team captain in my junior and senior seasons, too.

I am proud of what I accomplished, but as impressive as it sounds, those All-American certificates came from relays. Any time I swam an individual event in a high-pressure competition, I choked.

I always found a way to show up for my teammates in the relays, but I never figured out how to show up for myself.

Walking in as an underdog, I didn't have any pressure on me. But when I started to get good in my sophomore season, I started to feel the pressure. That pressure slowly took me down. I had no idea how to handle all the failures that were mounting up, and my fears and doubts controlled me. My senior season was my worst. I graduated and retired from the sport angry, frustrated, and just plain sad.

I had always wanted to be a coach, but I needed a break. It didn't last long. Less than a year later, I started my coaching career.

I coached two years at the club level, and then I moved to the college ranks. I was an assistant coach at Michigan State for two years, and at Southern Methodist University for four more, before becoming the head coach at the University of Miami in 2006.

As I look back on my first few years as a head coach, the only way I can define them is tumultuous. I failed miserably.

When I was an assistant at SMU, our program was one of the best in the country. I had the honor of coaching Olympians, world champions, and NCAA champions. I absolutely loved my job, and the team was like my family.

The head coach and I had a great relationship because we were complete opposites. He loved writing workouts and working on technique. His mind thought swimming 24/7. I, on the other hand, loved my relationships with the women and helping them with their confidence, mental health, and life outside of sport. He took care of the swimming. I took care of the women. And it worked beautifully.

I walked out of SMU knowing I was really good at what I do. I was a confident coach.

When I became a head coach, though, I thought that I had to take care of the swimming and leave the relationship part to my assistant. That's how it usually works. And I'm embarrassed to say that it took me four years to realize that wasn't working in my program. I knew something wasn't working, but I was blaming everyone but myself for the failures. I was miserable, my team didn't like me, and I absolutely hated my job. I wanted to quit.

Thankfully, I didn't. And thankfully, my ego finally broke, and I realized I couldn't keep doing the same thing and expect a different result. So, the summer before my fifth season, I found some mentors and started working on myself.

One of the first questions that my mentors asked me was what was I really good at. I didn't have an answer for them. I had been failing so miserably for four years that I couldn't even remember what I was good at. So they asked me what had made me such a great assistant coach.

That was easy. I took care of the women and their confidence.

They challenged me to do that again. "But that's not what head coaches do," I said.

They told me that I could continue to do what I thought a head coach was supposed to do, or I could start using my gifts.

I'm so thankful I took their challenge.

In my fifth season, I hired an assistant coach who thought sport 24/7, and I started taking care of the women. I gave my athletes an hour a week when they could come into my office and talk. Some days it was a 10-minute check-in. Some days it was a mental breakdown with tears and lots of tissues. Either way, it was their safe space to come in, be their authentic selves, and speak truth. They knew they could bare their souls with no judgment. I didn't call it "confidence coaching" back then, but that's exactly what I was doing.

I now had healthy, confident women on my team, and it completely changed my program. We started having a lot of success, I loved the women on my team, and I really enjoyed my job again.

But I realized that my passion wasn't swimming—it was the women and their confidence. So, in 2013, I left my coaching career with the intention of starting a business as a confidence coach and speaker.

But after 15 years of coaching, I ended up spending the next year just resting my soul.

I got pulled back into the swimming world for a year by working with a group called Team Elite. It was a group of national team swimmers and Olympians. I was back as an assistant swim coach, but most importantly, I was a confidence coach for the women as they prepared for the 2016 Olympic Trials and Olympic Games.

After leaving Team Elite, I started my business, Coach Christen, in 2016. When I started the business, I knew I wanted to make women my priority because women so often are *not* the priority. It has been my honor to work with some of the best female athletes in the world as a confidence coach, and to speak about confidence to female athletes and women in business.

Everything I'll be teaching you over the next 30 days comes from 20-plus years of women allowing me into the darkest parts of their souls. I feel so grateful that they trusted me enough to share their deepest insecurities, fears, traumas, hopes, and tears.

We will dive deep into how to build confidence, trust that confidence, and then use it to be successful. We will explore subjects like fear, comparing, perfectionism, unhealthy body image, and much more.

For the next 30 days, plan to reserve 15-20 minutes a day to work on your confidence. Each day in this book contains a short story or lesson and some additional thoughts and questions for you. I will plant the seed with the lesson, and your job is to water that seed by doing the work. As I tell my clients, I can share everything I know with you, but if you aren't willing to do the work, nothing will change.

Let me warn you—the work isn't always going to be easy. I challenge you to get vulnerable and be honest. I have left a journal page for writing after each lesson, but if you feel you'll need more space or don't want to write in this book, keep a separate journal throughout these 30 days.

I want you to look at your journal as "truth paper." You are not allowed to lie, sugarcoat, or water down your truth. Only 100% truth can be written on it.

I know that getting honest can be scary, but I have learned that real confidence always revolves around truth. Faking it, lying, sugarcoating, or watering down the truth never leads to real confidence. I've also learned that you find real confidence when you have nothing left to hide. So, no hiding. Only truth.

Take note: Some days will hit a little deeper and you'll want to spend a lot of time on them. Please make sure to take the time to do the work on all of the lessons, because you'll want to keep the information in your back pocket for the future.

Let's get to work!

DAY 1

FINALLY, THE TRUTH!

Day 1! I'm proud of you for showing up! This isn't always going to be easy, but I promise you, it will be worth it.

Over the next several days, you will learn how to handle fear and doubts.

But first, a story.

I was recruiting a possible transfer swimmer named Kelsi. She had been one of the fastest sprinters in the country out of high school and had been recruited by colleges like crazy. She had picked her dream school and walked into college full of hope and huge expectations. But only two years later, she was declaring her intent to transfer.

She wasn't getting faster. None of her expectations had been met, and after two years of failing, she had lost hope.

As she told me about her college experience thus far, tears ran down her face. Her story was common and familiar: she believed she could do something great, but it was just not happening. She was stuck, which is one of the most frustrating feelings in the world.

Coaching for as long as I had, I knew that talent doesn't just go away. I knew something was keeping her stuck, and I believed she could be great again. I believed she could be faster than ever.

Kelsi transferred to my program, and the first few weeks were magic. She showed up and gave everything she had. She was my favorite kind of athlete—a blue-collar scrapper. She was there every day and worked her ass off. You could see her confidence building.

Before long, we started racing her off the blocks after practice to see where her times stood, and we were all excited that she was faster than she had been in two years. Her confidence was through the roof.

She. Was. Back.

But then competitions began. And with competition comes pressure.

Pressure seems to change everything.

At our first swim meet, this confident woman was suddenly unsure of herself. She was hanging around the coaches asking a lot of questions, and she wasn't even sure what to do for warmup. I asked her if she was OK, and all I got in response was, "I'm fine."

Throughout the entire warmup, "I'm fine."

But I knew she wasn't.

She walked up to her first event unsure of herself, and it didn't go well. She not only lost to a rival, but she went slower than she had been going in practice. She came to me afterward on the verge of tears.

I told her that we could talk about that race later, but she needed to get ready for her next one. I told her to try to let it go—I believed in her, and the next race would go better.

She walked away with her head down and jumped into the warm-down pool. After five minutes, I started looking for her and found her bawling her eyes out.

In that moment, I knew that that race hadn't been just a slow time for her. In that losing moment, her hope had died.

She had walked into this new program—my program—with a new hope. She had allowed herself to dream that things would be different. Hope is a choice, after all, and she had made the courageous decision to hope and not just to go numb in survival mode.

But that first race showed her that nothing had changed. The tears were back, and her confidence evaporated.

After that first competition, every race got slower and slower.

I knew that we had to get to the bottom of this, so I set up a meeting with her. She came into my office only wanting to blame and complain. She had told me that at her old program, the training and coaching weren't right, the weight-room workouts weren't right, her teammates weren't positive enough, and so on, and now all those things were wrong with my program, too. I listened and recognized that she was doing what most people do when they are failing—looking for someone or something to blame besides themselves.

Though I was feeling defensive about my program, I stayed quiet, and I let her vent. I've learned that getting things off your chest can be therapeutic. I did try to interrupt a couple times to ask about her confidence, but it was as if a big wall blocked that train of thought. She was not willing to go there.

After the meeting, I could tell that she felt lighter. I asked her if she'd like to continue to meet, and because she was feeling so much better, she accepted.

A lot of the meetings continued to be full of blaming and complaining; but slowly, she started to trust me, and I could tell that her wall was starting to crack.

During one of our meetings, I asked her this question: "What are you thinking when you are behind the blocks getting ready to race?"

For swimmers, behind the blocks is the scariest place in the world. The spotlight is on you, and the pressure to perform is on.

She closed her eyes and thought about it, and then she said these three things out loud:

"What if I lose?"

"What if I don't go fast?"

"What if I'm just not as good as I think I am?"

Her eyes jolted open. She was in shock. She didn't intend to get that honest with me—it was just one of those vulnerable moments that fell out of her mouth.

But more importantly, she surprised herself because she didn't realize those thoughts were going through her mind until that moment.

She said she didn't remember when those thoughts started, but she knew that, whenever they did, she tried really hard to squash them. To her, no elite athlete should have those kinds of thoughts. She had been taught to be "mentally tough," so she shoved those questions down, pretended they weren't there, and hoped they'd someday go away.

But they didn't go away. Slowly, by ignoring them, they became a normal part of her pre-race routine. It was as if they were programmed into her, and she didn't even know it. She was diving into her races with those thoughts leading the way.

I started to understand why she had been stuck for so long.

When I start working with a client, they often tell me that they're nervous and feel fear and anxiety before or during their competitions. When I ask what's going through their mind, a common answer I hear is, "I don't know."

Well, if you don't know, you can't fix it.

Here's the truth: It's time to wake up! Be aware of your thoughts, and stop avoiding the scary, embarrassing, or "weak" thoughts. They could be leading the way as you walk into your competitions.

Do the work:

How did this lesson make you feel?

Could you relate?

A good place to start waking up is at practice. Pay attention to your thoughts, and after practice, write them down. Don't be shocked or beat yourself up if they are negative. I promise you, you're not alone. Don't sugarcoat. If you're not honest, you can't fix it.

Unsure of where to start? Here are some prompts:

What are you thinking

        ... during practice?

        ... after you make a mistake?

        ... when you're behind?

        ... when you have a challenge in front of you?

        ... when it gets really hard?

        ... when you're having a bad practice?

        ... when you're having a great practice?

        ... when Coach yells at you or critiques you?

DAY 2

THE WHAT IFS

"What if I lose?"

"What if I don't go fast?"

"What if I'm not as good as I think I am?"

Maybe those questions sound familiar to you. I know they did to me.

I graduated from college and retired from swimming in 1997, but I can still remember the fear I felt behind the blocks with those "what ifs" racing through my mind.

I thought I was weak. I thought there was something wrong with me. I thought I was failing miserably at being mentally tough. I thought all my teammates and competitors were fearless, and I was the weakling of my team.

And because I didn't want anyone to know that I was the weakling, I stayed quiet.

But in the years since, here's what I've learned about fear: everyone experiences it, yet everyone also thinks they are alone in that experience.

When we feel like we are the only one, we wonder, *What is wrong with me?* And because we fear that something is wrong with us, we are definitely not going to admit our fear or talk about it. So we stay quiet and suffer alone.

Many years ago, I asked a group of teenage athletes to write what they thought in their pressure-to-perform moments. As I passed out the paper, I told them to write anonymously because I knew they might not be completely honest if they had to put their names on it.

When it was time to hand them in, the athletes folded their pieces of paper so many times that I was getting back tiny, little squares. They did not want anyone to see what they had written.

I finished our meeting and got in my car; then I unfolded the papers and read them.

As I read, my first thought was that I wanted to bawl my eyes out. I couldn't believe the terror that was folded into these pieces of paper.

It didn't take me long to realize how common this was.

I started asking female athletes from all sports and from every level, from beginners to Olympians: "What are you thinking in your pressure-to-perform moments?"

Almost universally, the answers are exactly what I saw that day with those teenagers; really scary stuff. And yes, even from those women whom we watch on TV and think, *I wish I could be fearless like them.*

Over the years, I've collected a list of the top answers that I hear from athletes when I ask that question. Some differ slightly because of the amount of pressure, but for the most part, they are pretty similar:

"What if all my hard work doesn't pay off? What if I give my all, sacrifice, and do everything right, and it still doesn't pay off?"

"What if it hurts?"

"What if I disappoint my coach, my parents, my team, my fans?"

"What if I embarrass myself?"

"What if I get beat?"

"What if I mess up and don't get my job done?"

"What if my team/coach gets frustrated with me?"

"What if I can't finish strong?"

"What if I'm out of my league? What if I don't belong here?"

"What if I don't get recruited?"

"What if I don't deserve this?"

"What if I'm not prepared?"

"What if I'm not good enough?"

"What if it happens again?"

I hear this one a lot, as well: "I let my confidence be controlled by my first couple of plays. If they're good, then I'm good. But if I mess up or do something dumb, I struggle with confidence for the entire game. So, basically, going into a game, I get anxious because I feel like my performance is a toss-up."

That's a lot of What Ifs. And here's where it gets even trickier:

If we ignore the What Ifs long enough, the What If goes away. Great! Right?

No.

"What if I'm not good enough?" turns into "I'm not good enough."

"What if I'm out of my league?" turns into "I am out of my league."

I share these with you because if you've ever had thoughts like this, know that you are 100% normal. There is nothing wrong with you. It doesn't mean you're weak, it doesn't mean you're a head case, and it certainly doesn't mean that you can't be confident.

When I speak to teams, without fail, there is someone wiping tears when I say this. It is such a relief to know there's nothing wrong, and you are not alone. Even the best athletes in the world have these thoughts, too.

Here's the truth:

You're not weak or a head case. You're afraid, and that's OK.

Do the work:

How did this lesson make you feel?

Could you relate?

It's important to note that when everything is going right, there's not much to be afraid of. But when failure and disappointment enter the equation, a lot of fear does, too.

I worked with an Olympian who had a lot of success as a teenager and didn't struggle much with fear. She admits there were a couple doubts, but she didn't really fear failing, because she hadn't yet. But then she got stuck, and a lot of failures added up.

After the failures, the fears came like a tidal wave. When I challenged her to get honest about her What Ifs, she came up with three pages' worth.

So younger athletes reading this may not fully grasp the What Ifs, yet. But those who have experienced failure can expect to write a lot.

What are your pressure-to-perform moments?

What are you thinking in those moments?

Start your own list of What If's. Some of these might be easy to think about, and you probably already know what they are. But there are others that maybe you've avoided, and it might take a little longer to realize these. Start your list, stay awake and aware, and keep adding to your list as thoughts pop up.

DAY 3

FAKE IT 'TIL YOU MAKE IT?

Before Kelsi admitted her What Ifs, I consistently asked her how she felt. Every time, all she said was, "I'm fine. I'm fine. I'm fine."

I didn't know it then, but I can see now that she was breaking out her inner tap dancer.

I believe every woman has a tap dancer inside. Women are supposed to be perfect, and we certainly don't want anyone to know that we're not. So, when life isn't going well, the stress and fear are mounting, and people are noticing that we're cracking, we start "tap dancing" and performing with a fake smile on our face, telling everyone that we are "fine."

For many years, Kelsi avoided her fear and bought into the idea that if she tap-danced and faked it, she'd somehow make it. She believed that if she faked being confident and told everyone that she was "fine," that would lead her into someday "making it."

But there are two problems with that kind of thinking.

First, there's a big difference between appearing confident and actually being confident.

I envision fear as a big, colorful bird, and it's flapping its wings and chirping loudly, making so much noise, there's no way anyone could miss it. It's hanging out on your shoulder, and it's chirping fears and What Ifs into your ear.

The way most athletes learn to handle fear is to turn their head away from the bird and pretend it is not there: "I don't see you. I'm fine."

But just because you fake that you're fine doesn't mean that you are. And just because you pretend that fear is not there, doesn't mean that it's not there. And it certainly doesn't mean that it's not affecting you in a negative way.

If you walk into a competition with those fears and What Ifs swirling through your mind, you have no shot of reaching your fullest potential.

You think you are acting tough by faking it and avoiding the fear, but the truth is that it takes much more courage to wake up and own it:

"I see you, What-If-I-Disappoint-Everyone."

"I see you, What-If-I-Embarrass-Myself."

"I see you, What-If-I-Fail."

But I get it. Avoidance is easier. We're supposed to be mentally tough, so let's fake it and shove the fear down, and hope that it will go away.

Second problem: It doesn't just go away.

For so many years, Kelsi avoided the fears and doubts because she was embarrassed. She felt everyone around her was fearless, and she didn't want to admit that she wasn't. So she shoved those fears down into the darkness, hoping they'd go away. But they didn't go away; they became like an anchor in her. She'd try to take a step forward, but the anchor kept her stuck.

And because she was stuck, the failures kept adding up, and that anchor got heavier and heavier.

After Kelsi admitted her initial What Ifs, she realized there was a lot more that she'd been hiding. Meeting after meeting, she was finally speaking the truth, and she felt so much freedom. It's hard work to fake it. She felt like a weight had been lifted from her when she was able to be real and she didn't have to tap dance anymore. She was finally able to be herself.

It's important to note, too, that Kelsi didn't have to take a megaphone and tell the world. She told one person her truth, and she was finally free. When she was free from the anchor, she was free to walk forward into her potential.

Here's the truth: When you have to fake it, you don't actually make it.

Do the work:

How did this lesson make you feel?

Could you relate?

Have you been tap dancing?

Do you find yourself faking it?

Are you starting to realize it's hard work to fake it?

What is in your anchor?

Are you ready to speak truth and get real?

DAY 4

REAL AND POSITIVE

Let's take some time to talk about being positive. Many of us look at positivity like a light switch. We can go from a grumpy, negative, fearful woman, to "Flip the switch! Yay! I'm so positive and happy, and life is full of rainbows and cotton candy!"

I wish it could be that easy, but that is not realistic. Flipping the switch leads you into faking it and acting like all is "fine." And we've learned that faking it never leads to making it. It's time to be real.

I was working with a college athlete who was struggling with motivation at a competition. It had fallen in the middle of a really hard training cycle and midterms, so she was exhausted and worn down. She went to her coaches to explain to them her struggle, and they responded with, "Just be positive!"

At the time, she looked at being positive as a light switch, and she tried her best. But she just couldn't find the motivation. Then, because she was failing at the positivity, she started to beat herself up and wonder, *What's wrong with me that I can't be positive?*

Luckily, she made the wise decision to find a quiet place and call me. She was almost in tears, because she was cold and tired and didn't want to be there. She explained her dilemma that she couldn't find any positivity, and I asked her, "You'd rather be in bed watching Netflix, right?"

And she said, "I'd love to be in bed watching Netflix!"

"That's OK," I said. "You're allowed to feel that way. But here's a truth I know about you: You are not the type of woman who is ever going to walk into a competition and not give 100 percent. Right?"

"Of course! I would never not give 100 percent," she said. "But wait, I'm allowed to feel this way?"

"Of course, you are," I told her. "The truth is, you're exhausted and worn down. But here's your reality: You are at a competition. And you're not the type of woman who would ever give mediocre effort."

She felt relieved that there wasn't something wrong with her because she was feeling this way. She was relieved that she wasn't just being negative because she wasn't feeling motivated. But she also embraced her reality and figured out how to be her best and give her best *in that situation*. She gave herself a chance to have a great competition.

I think about how the competition would have ended if she had kept beating herself up because she couldn't be positive. I suspect it wouldn't have gone well.

Life is not full of rainbows and cotton candy, and you certainly know sport isn't, either. You are allowed to be real, but you must also embrace reality and ask yourself, "How do I be my best and give my best in this situation?"

How about when your first play doesn't go well, you make a mistake, or you have a bad race? A lot of you are going to get advice that revolves around staying positive and just trying to let it go. Don't you love it when people tell you to "just let it go"? I've noticed that most women don't easily let things go.

Don't try to flip the switch and find rainbows and cotton candy. You're allowed to be real: "I'm disappointed. This is not how I wanted to start things. This is not ideal. But it is my reality, so how can I be my best and give my best moving forward?"

And what about injuries? They're always a shock, because they are never a part of the plan. You are allowed to be frustrated and sad and cry your eyes out. And when you are ready, it's time to start thinking, "How can I be my best and give my best in this unplanned new reality?"

A lot of your practices and competitions aren't going to go smoothly, and things aren't always going to go your way. There will be times you walk in and you don't want to be there. There will be times that you don't perform well. There will be times that nothing seems to go right. There will be times that injury completely changes your plans. But you can choose to be both real and positive: "This is not ideal, and this is not what I want, but it is my reality. How do I be my best and give my best in this moment?"

Here's the truth: You are allowed to be real and positive.

Do the work:

How did this lesson make you feel?

Could you relate?

Do you try to flip the switch?

Do you find yourself faking it when you're trying to be positive?

How can you be real and positive?

How can you positively respond to the advice of "Just be positive" without falling into the "flip the switch" trap?

Think of a few strategies that will allow you to respond in a way that is positive for you.

DAY 5

TEMPER TANTRUMS

When Kelsi finally admitted her What Ifs, our first thought was that she needed to get rid of them. Her What Ifs were causing fear and doubts and keeping her stuck. Obviously, they must go!

But there was a big problem. No matter how hard she tried, those What Ifs kept showing up. Whenever she felt pressure, they came back, every time.

I realized that we had to come up with a better plan than just hoping they would go away. The new plan needed to include learning how to handle fear when it comes. Kelsi needed to realize that if she were always going to "go there" in her mind, she at least didn't have to stay there.

I don't believe in being fearless when you are under pressure. If you have expectations for yourself and there is something at stake, I believe fears are coming every single time.

So, like Kelsi, you're gonna go there. You just can't stay there. So, let's figure out how to break free.

We'll start with the basics and look at the What Ifs.

Every time you walk into a competition, you risk failure. This is one of the hardest parts of being in sport. There are no guarantees, and you don't know what's going to happen. You are vulnerable, and vulnerability is always uncomfortable.

Unknowns are unpredictable, and you hate not knowing what's going to happen. You want to control it all! You are desperate to feel at least a little bit of control in these scary situations.

Feeling uncomfortable with no control, you start trying to predict the outcome of the competition. Thinking you may know the outcome, you feel a little less vulnerable and a little more comfortable. You feel like you have at least a little control over this very scary moment.

But you don't.

Additionally, in my experience, when women try to predict the outcome, they almost always go to the worst-case scenario. I don't know anyone walking into a competition seriously thinking, *What if this is the greatest moment of my life? What if everything goes right today?*

Don't get me wrong, you probably try. You try to think positively and say to yourself, *I got this. I can do this. I will be great today.*

But your next thoughts are, *But what if I don't got this?* And then you go down a rabbit hole of imagined worst-case scenarios.

Before the competition even begins, you see yourself fail. You see yourself finish disappointed and frustrated. You see yourself mess up and be the reason your team loses.

And when you walk into a competition already seeing yourself fail, you're not giving yourself a chance to succeed.

You cannot predict the future. You are not a psychic. You are not a fortune teller. You cannot predict what hasn't happened yet. It's vulnerability or bust. You're either all in and leaning into the uncomfortable vulnerability, or you're all out. There's no in-between.

I was working with an Olympian who would fall into the prediction trap. She hated feeling like she had no control. She would go worst-case scenario and throw herself into a panic. Her body would tighten from the fear, and she would walk into competitions fearing the worst.

I reminded her that she is not a psychic, and she cannot predict the future. Her response? She clenched her fists and pounded the table saying, "But I want to know! I want to know! I want to know!"

She was half laughing and half crying.

Sound familiar? Gosh, wouldn't it be so nice to just know how it's going to go? It would relieve so much fear, pressure, and stress. But unfortunately, the future hasn't happened yet. It is unknown.

You have two choices in this situation. You can have a temper tantrum and pound the table with clenched fists, or you can accept the truth that you cannot predict. You must lean into the vulnerability and embrace that you don't know what's going to happen. Yes, there's a chance of failure. That's the risk you take in sports. But you're either leaning into vulnerability all in, or you're all out. Again, there's no in-between.

That Olympian made a plan. Before her competitions, she would clench her fists as hard as she could to remind herself that she can have a temper tantrum if she wants. But she can also release her hands and embrace that she doesn't know what is going to happen. That allowed her to release everything she could not control in that moment. She was all in.

Now remember, accepting that you can't predict doesn't mean that you won't try to do it anyway. Your job is to know when you are predicting and pull yourself into the present and what you know in the moment.

Can you imagine the power you'd have if you could walk into a competition saying, "I don't know what's about to happen, but I do know that I'm all in"?

Here's the truth: You cannot predict the future. It's vulnerability or bust.

Do the work:

How did this lesson make you feel?

Could you relate?

Do you struggle with being vulnerable?

Do you think you are walking into competitions already seeing the worst-case scenario?

Do you find yourself tight as you walk into competitions?

Do you need to unclench your fists and admit that you do not know the future?

How can you be all in?

DAY 6

DOWN DEEP

As a woman with a million thoughts going through her mind, you wouldn't think that one thought out of the million could be the wrecking ball that takes out your confidence. But I've learned that when those What Ifs start coming, it's as if we take a flashlight and shine it on those fears alone. Those fears are our focus.

So how do you get from those worst-case scenario thoughts that bring so much fear and anxiety to something that's going to allow you to perform at your potential?

The logical answer is to flip that flashlight from your What Ifs and fears and shine it onto something more positive—something that allows you to believe this performance will go well. Maybe something like a positive affirmation.

But I've run into a major problem with this activity.

Many athletes have told me that from a young age, they have been taught to stand before their competition and say these positive affirmations: "I got this! I will be great today! I will be fast today! I will score today! I will reach my goals!"

But there was always a problem. Down deep, they didn't actually believe any of it.

I believe that women are way too smart to con themselves into believing something that they don't actually believe. A woman's down-deep seems to always tell her the truth.

What you focus on, you must truly believe.

I was working with a long-distance runner who got to start at the front of her race because she was one of the fastest runners in the field.

The race began, and she was hanging with all the other fast runners. But then, about halfway through the race, the other runners started to pull away from her.

She tried to stay positive and told herself, *Just relax. You can still catch them.*

Over and over, she told herself positive affirmations.

But she had a terrible race, and she was physically and emotionally exhausted by the end.

When we talked, I told her to go back to the moment when she was telling herself to relax because she could still catch them.

I asked her, "Did you actually believe that you could catch them?"

Within half a second, I got back a, "Hell, no!"

She was faking it. No matter how hard she tried to con herself, she didn't believe it.

It takes energy to con yourself. That's why this runner was so emotionally drained on top of being physically spent.

This runner is one of the hardest workers in her sport. She's that blue-collar scrapper who shows up every day and works her butt off. It isn't hard to find something she can believe.

I asked her, "What's your truth? "What's something that you could have focused on in that moment that you truly believed?"

She thought about it and said, "The truth is, I don't know if I can catch them because I have zero control over anyone else. But without a doubt, I know that I will always show up, and I will always fight. I am a fighter."

She knew that, without a doubt. That is a truth she didn't have to con herself into.

I have another client, a soccer player, who would find herself beating herself up after a mistake during a game. *What if it happens again? What if my mistakes cause my team to lose? What if? What if? What if?*

She was taught to keep telling herself, *It will be ok. I got this.*

Over and over, *I got this.*

I asked her, "Do you really believe you 'got this'?"

She was quick to answer, "Of course not." She was too busy dreading that the mistake meant the entire game was going to be bad for her.

It didn't matter how many times she said it. She had to find something to focus on that she truly believed down deep.

So, I asked her, "What is something that you believe about yourself?"

She couldn't answer right away, so I gave her a week. When she came back, she said:

"I know that I am determined and resilient. I always get back up.

"I am a hard worker, and I know I will continue to work.

"I am a fighter, and I know I will continue to fight."

Now, after a mistake, she can put her focus on her truth, and get her head back in the game quickly.

Let's not forget, though, that focusing on truth without interruption is unrealistic. Go to truth, and when a What If tries to throw you off, it's your job to pull yourself back.

But what if? Pull yourself back to truth.

But what if? Pull yourself back to truth.

And here's the great news: The more you pull yourself back to truth, the easier it gets.

Here's the truth: When the What Ifs come, you must focus on the truth that you believe down deep. Then continue to pull yourself back to truth.

Do the work:

How did that lesson make you feel?

Could you relate?

Have you ever tried to con yourself into believing, "I got this," when down deep you didn't believe it?

What are some things that you tell yourself when you're feeling fear?

What's a truth that you believe about yourself down deep?

This may take a while, and that's OK. You don't have to have the answer today. Take some time to think about it.

DAY 7

UNCOMFORTABLE IN TRUTH

When I asked my soccer player her truth and she didn't know, it didn't surprise me. In my experience, a lot of women have a hard time with their truth. I've noticed that many women are uncomfortable in their truth.

When I do a team-building talk, I like to break up the team into smaller groups of six, and each group makes a circle. Then, with the attention on one person in the group, the other five tell her what she's great at and what she brings to the team. They then focus on the next person and repeat the exercise. As they go around the circle, everyone hears from the other five people in their group.

I then bring the team back together and ask each woman to say out loud what they heard their teammates tell them.

You'd think I'd asked them to say it in front of a live TV audience of millions. The women are always extremely uncomfortable as they say their truth.

I hear them nervously say things like:

"I heard I'm a good teammate."

"I'm a hard worker."

"I'm always there to listen when someone needs to talk."

"I help keep the team positive and motivated."

"I make people laugh."

And so on, but they seem really embarrassed to talk about it.

After they say what they heard from their teammates, I then ask them if they agree with what they heard. This is where it gets really awkward. They can hardly look me in the eye when they quietly say, "Yes."

I tell them, "If you agree, then own it. Say it proudly."

This is when a couple of the women will come out of their shell and say it proudly, but the majority say it just as uncomfortably as the first time.

What they heard was not surprising to them. Of course, they know what they're great at. We all do. Yet they practically go into distress having to admit it out loud.

Over the years, it's become clear to me that most women are incredibly uncomfortable in their truth. They're uncomfortable talking about themselves, talking about their accomplishments, and talking about their gifts.

That's why a three-time Olympian client of mine said, "How embarrassing," when she had an article written about her, and the first page listed all of her accomplishments.

And it's why I hear watered-down truths like:

"I don't mean to sound cocky, but I'm a really hard worker."

"I don't want you to think I'm arrogant, but I'm a warrior in practice."

"I don't want to brag, but I feel like I have a lot of talent."

So, why are so many women uncomfortable in their truths?

I believe it starts with unconscious gender bias.

A man is called a leader while women are called controlling or bossy. A man is "angry" while women are "hysterical." A man is applauded for his ambition while a woman is looked down on for being "overly ambitious."

And a confident man is admired while a confident woman is seen as arrogant, cocky, or bragging. A confident man gets a standing ovation while a confident woman gets eye rolls with a "Who does she think she is?"

To avoid the eye rolls, you might have learned to shrink back and shut up. You might have learned to water down your truth.

You may not think it's a big deal, but when you are in your pressure-to-perform moment and you are desperate for truth, watered-down truth ain't gonna get the job done.

Real confidence always revolves around truth, not watered-down truth.

Embrace your truth. It's not cocky, arrogant, or bragging. It's truth.

Here's the truth: To find real confidence, you must embrace and get comfortable in your truth.

Do the work:

How did this lesson make you feel?

Could you relate?

What are you great at? What do you bring to your team?

Are you uncomfortable in your truth?

Do you water down your truth? Do you catch yourself adding, "I don't mean to sound cocky" or something similar to your truth?

Do you have a hard time talking about yourself or your accomplishments? Why?

Can you think of times that you have made yourself "less" accomplished or downplayed your abilities to avoid the eye rolls?

DAY 8

A MILLION THOUGHTS

Client: I had a really bad game. I played terribly the whole time.

Me: OK. What was going through your mind?

Client: I don't think I was thinking anything.

Me: WRONG!

Client thinks on it: I guess after I screwed up my first play, I started freaking out, thinking, "What if this is going to be a horrible game for me?"

Client: About halfway through my race, I started to struggle physically. It really hurt.

Me: What was going through your mind?

Client: I don't think I was thinking anything.

Me: WRONG!

Client thinks on it: I was thinking about how much pain I was in. I was thinking, "Ouch, this isn't going to turn out well."

Client: When I walked up to bat, I was having a lot of anxiety and started to panic.

Me: What was going through your mind?

Client: I don't think I was thinking anything.

Me: WRONG!

Client thinks on it: I was thinking about what a head case I am.

Had these women kept believing they weren't thinking about anything, they never would have been able to change anything. They would have assumed they weren't thinking about anything and would have missed out on their chance to flip their focus to their truth.

The best way I describe a woman's brain is beautiful chaos. I think most women can agree that their minds are usually full of a million thoughts. They never seem to be simple thoughts, either. They're usually pretty deep and complex. No matter how badly you might need a break from thinking, your brain never seems to turn off.

If that isn't chaos enough, add in emotions, and the chaos doesn't always seem so beautiful. I would guess that you've been called an overthinker on more than one occasion.

Yet…

Every Client: I'm feeling really nervous and anxious walking into competitions.

Me: What do you usually do when you start feeling anxious?

Every Client: I try not to think about anything.

You should assume that you are thinking something at all times. You should assume your brain doesn't turn off. You should assume you don't have the luxury of thinking about nothing.

But unfortunately, there are a lot of women who have gotten bad advice that revolves around trying not to think.

I worked with a swimmer who was having a lot of fear and anxiety behind the blocks. Her coach told her, "If behind the blocks is scary for you, don't go behind the blocks too early. Instead of standing up there waiting for your race, you should go into the warm-down pool, swim easy, and don't think about anything.

"Then when your race is up, run up there, get on the blocks, and go!"

If only things were so beautifully simple.

I told her to try it, but I also challenged her to wake up and be aware of her thoughts in every location.

As I'm sure you've already guessed, she told me that she was thinking the exact same things in the warm-down pool as she was behind the blocks.

Of course, she was. Changing locations wasn't going to turn off her brain.

Had I not intervened, she would have tried to think about nothing, failed, and then beat herself up, wondering why she's such an "overthinker."

But because she stayed aware of her thoughts in every location, she was able to pull herself into truth and have a great competition.

Your brain is beautiful chaos. Trying not to think about it or trying to turn your brain off is probably not going to be much help. Stay awake and aware of your thoughts at all times, so you can get yourself back to truth.

Here's the truth: It's safe to assume that you are thinking something at all times.

Do the work:

How did this lesson make you feel?

Could you relate?

Have you ever gotten advice to stop overthinking?

Have you ever gotten advice to not think at all?

Do you find yourself trying to think about nothing?

DAY 9

ACTIVATE THE ANGEL

In the beautiful chaos of your brain, do you ever feel like you have several voices within you? Do they sometimes seem to be at war with each other?

The most powerful voice seems to love the What Ifs, every worst-case scenario, and telling you your goals are not possible. The weaker voice tries to throw some positivity at that other voice, but the powerful one usually wins.

With a brain full of a million thoughts, you can come up with a lot of worst-case scenarios and reasons you won't succeed. And when you start thinking about everything that could go wrong, a tidal wave of fear hits, and it's very easy to panic. In panic, it feels as if your brain shuts down, and the panic leads you to start believing things that aren't true.

For example, I have a three-time Olympian for a client who has been doing her sport for 20-plus years, who walks into a competition, and the minute she starts to panic, she starts to believe she doesn't know what she's doing.

She's been playing her sport for more than two decades; she's one of the best in the world, and she doesn't know what she's doing? Really?

That's the power of panic.

Think about the old belief that you have an angel on one shoulder and a devil on the other. The devil is a negative voice that tries its best to lead you down the wrong path. The angel is there to speak some positivity and lead you the other way.

When you panic, you are giving power to the devil to lead you down the wrong path. The angel sits quiet while the devil has its way. All the negativity, all the fears, all the doubts, all the nonsense, is all you seem to hear.

It is your job to activate the angel. It is your job to be aware of what you are hearing, and then speak truth and perspective to the lies.

A client of mine was at an international competition. She knew that if she started to freak out from the pressure, she could call me for help with finding some perspective and truth.

Unfortunately, the competition began when it was about 3 a.m., my time. She didn't want to wake me up, so she sent me a text saying, "I'm activating the angel."

Then she sent another text of all the lies panic was creating, and the truth and perspective that she spoke to those lies.

Panic: You don't know what you're doing.

Truth: Of course, I know what I'm doing. I've done thousands of practices. I've done hundreds of competitions. I am brilliant at my sport.

Panic: You're a lot tougher in practice than you are at competitions.

Truth: There aren't two versions of me. The same woman who is tough, works hard, and is a warrior in practice is the same woman walking into this competition.

Panic: This is going to be so hard.

Truth: Yep, of course, it's going to be hard. But I do hard every day. And I do hard really well.

Panic: You're a head case.

Truth: Just because I'm afraid doesn't make me a head case. I'm doing the work, and I know what to do to pull myself into truth.

Panic: You don't deserve this.

Truth: I deserve all the good stuff that comes from my hard work. I made the choice to work hard, and I deserve success.

Panic: You haven't worked hard enough.

Truth: Every time I've worked hard, it was like putting money in the bank. I haven't been perfect, but I've been consistent in giving my best. I'm walking into this competition a millionaire.

Panic: Everyone will be disappointed if you don't win or you don't reach your goal.

Truth: The only thing I can do is give my best effort. And the good news is that I give my best in practice every day. So, today, I'm going to do what I do every day.

Panic: The same thing is going to happen that always happens.

Truth: I've been doing the work, and I'm not the same woman I used to be.

When you are aware of your panic, and speak truth and perspective to it, it gives you your best chance to move forward and perform at your potential.

Here's the truth: It is your job to activate the angel and speak truth and perspective to the lies.

Do the work:

How did this lesson make you feel?

Could you relate?

What lies do you find yourself believing when you're in panic?

What is a truth you can speak to the lies?

It may be helpful to write down the lies on one side of the page and then the truth across from them.

DAY 10

GOOD TO GREAT

Over the last few days, we have talked a lot about pulling yourself into truth when the tidal wave of fear hits you. It's important to know that this is a journey, and pulling yourself into truth can look different on different occasions.

In late 2014, I was invited to speak to a swim club, and while I was there, I had a one-on-one with a young woman named Katie Meili. She was having major anxiety before her races, and she often felt paralyzed by the fear. At that time, Katie was a good swimmer, but not great. But she really wanted to be great.

After that meeting, we started working together and she got honest about her fears. She was a hard worker who took pride in doing things right, so inevitably, "What if all my hard work doesn't pay off?" was one of her big What Ifs.

Once she was aware of all of the fears swirling through her mind, she realized that she did not like how they felt inside of her. She felt that she needed to speak them out. She wanted to feel as if she were getting them out of her soul.

So, in the beginning, that's what she did. She spoke her fears out before her competitions. And because she learned that's what she needed to combat her fears, she got faster and faster. In 2015, she qualified for the U.S. National Team.

At her first international competition representing the United States, she was obviously feeling a lot of pressure. She had dreamed of this moment, but when her event was up, the tidal wave of fear started to overwhelm her. She started to panic, and she felt paralyzed.

After a few seconds of panicking, she reminded herself that she knew these fears were coming, and that she knew what to do—to speak those fears out. As she was thinking about what she needed to do, she saw one of her teammates walking toward the team area. She called her name and asked if she'd come behind the blocks with her.

Her teammate came over, and Katie said, "Don't say anything back; I just need to say this out loud:

"What if all my hard work doesn't pay off? What if I don't go a best time? What if I don't win? What if I disappoint everyone? What if I'm not ready?"

She said all her What Ifs out loud, and her teammate said, "OK!" and continued walking to the team area.

Katie stood up and won the gold. She also went the fastest time in the world that year.

There is no way that she would have been able to do that if she hadn't learned how to handle those fears when they came.

As excited as we were for her breakthrough, she had one more year until Olympic Trials. She stayed consistent working on her confidence, and after a few months, she realized that she didn't feel the need to speak her fears anymore.

She went back to her roots and started doing an activity that she used to do as a kid. Before every competition, she would write down 10 reasons why she was going to swim fast. Those ten reasons were her truths that she would focus on when the tidal wave of fear came.

At Olympic Trials, she stayed focused on her truth, and she made the 2016 U.S. Olympic team. I couldn't have been prouder. But I also knew that walking into the Olympic Games was going to bring another level of pressure. There were going to be tidal waves of fear in Rio. But I also felt confident that she would find a way to pull herself into truth.

She walked into prelims and semifinals with her 10 reasons why she was going to swim fast, and she made the finals. Oh, my! The finals at the Olympic Games! The eight fastest women in the world. Millions watching.

As she thought about the gravity of the moment during warmup for finals, the tidal wave of fear took her out. The tears started to flow. The pressure seemed unbearable, and she knew she had to speak.

She walked up to a coach and bawled to him. Luckily, she chose the right coach, and instead of telling her to "just be positive," he told her a lovely story about gratitude. It calmed her mind and made her start thinking about how grateful she was to be in this position. Gratitude was soothing her soul.

Her event was up, and she was called to the ready room. She felt so grateful to be sitting in the ready room at the Olympic Games, and she felt so grateful for the people that helped her get there.

As she was getting ready for the biggest race of her life, she made the decision to say out loud every person who had helped her get to this point in her career. Gratitude was her truth.

She got some weird looks because she was talking to herself, but she didn't care. She stayed focused on her gratefulness to everyone who had been a positive part of her journey.

Then, she stood up in front of millions and was able to give her best.

I bawled my eyes out as I watched her get on the medal podium to receive her bronze medal. After all the work she had put in physically and mentally, she undoubtedly deserved this.

All those years, the talent and hard work were there, but Katie's fears kept holding her back. When she decided to work on her fears, it changed everything for her. Though the process of how she handled the fear changed through her journey, she made sure that her confidence always revolved around truth. And by pulling herself into truth, she was finally able to reach her fullest potential.

Here's the truth: How you handle your fear may change on different occasions. As long as you are pulling yourself back to truth that you believe down deep, you give yourself your best chance to move forward from the fear and into your fullest potential.

Do the work:

How did this lesson make you feel?

Could you relate?

What part of Katie's story felt most relatable?

Do any of these strategies for handling your fears speak to you?

What's your truth that you will pull yourself into at your next competition?

DAY 11

NEVER GOOD ENOUGH

Another reason many women have a hard time with their truth is because they tend to struggle with giving themselves credit. For the next several days, we will be diving deep into why women don't give themselves credit, and how that can negatively affect confidence.

When I started working one-on-one with Kelsi, I watched her closely at practice and tried to validate her as much as possible. If she did something well, I would say something to let her know she was seen and that she did a great job.

I thought that would help her with her confidence.

Her response to my validation, though, was almost always, "Oh, please, it wasn't that big of a deal.

"It wasn't that good. It should have been better. It should have been faster."

Nothing ever seemed to be good enough or fast enough for her. Unless she did something extraordinary in practice, it was never good enough.

Around the same time, I was working with a professional basketball player who was very disciplined. She was so dedicated, always the last one to leave practice every day, and she did all the extras to get better.

Whenever I said something validating to her, her response was, "Oh, that's just me. That's just who I am."

Ummmmm, no. That's not just who you are.

That's hard work. That's dedication. That's sacrifice.

Once I saw this behavior in these two women, it opened my eyes, and I started to see it everywhere. Women struggle to give themselves credit.

I work with women who have big goals. They're always willing to work hard and take steps toward achieving those goals, but then they often struggle to give themselves credit for the steps that they are taking.

In their minds, it should have been better, it's never a big deal, and it is never enough. Besides, that's just them.

Another thing that I noticed was that my athletes could do 99 things right in practice and one thing wrong, and what do you think they were walking out thinking about? The one wrong thing. They never gave themselves credit for the 99 things they had done right, and they would leave practice upset about the one thing they did wrong.

For example, a client was in preseason and starting to do her annual fitness tests. She had spent the summer training, so she walked into these tests confident that she was going to kill it. And she did. But on the seventh of 12 stations, she didn't do as many pull-ups as she wanted.

She dominated the fitness tests, she was better than any of her teammates, yet she walked out beating herself up over station 7.

To feel confident, you must feel prepared, right? You must feel that you have done enough work to be your best in that particular moment.

But let me ask you this: If you never give yourself credit, and you are only focused on what you are doing wrong, how are you ever going to feel prepared?

Think about it. If you never give yourself credit because nothing is ever good enough, and you never pay attention to things you are doing well, you will never feel prepared. You will doubt that you are ready for the moment.

You must start giving yourself the credit you deserve.

As I thought about how to help women give themselves the credit they deserve, I envisioned confidence as gold nuggets.

Every time you work hard and take a step toward your goals, and then actually give yourself credit and admit, "I made the choice to do it, and I deserve credit," you gain a gold nugget.

Take a step, give yourself credit, gain a gold nugget. Take a step, give yourself credit, gain a gold nugget. Pay attention to the 99 things you're doing well, gain gold nuggets.

Keep building all of those gold nuggets, so by the time you walk into a competition, you can walk in with a mountain of gold nuggets.

No matter how many times the tidal wave of fear tries to lead you into believing you are not prepared, the gold nuggets are proof that you've done the work and you are ready for the moment.

Here's the truth: To feel confident and prepared, you must start giving yourself credit for the steps that you are taking and the hard work that you are putting in.

Do the work:

How did this lesson make you feel?

Could you relate?

Are you realizing you may not be giving yourself credit?

When you get a compliment or validation, how do you respond? Do you just say, "Thank you"?

Do you walk out of practice thinking about what you did well or the things you did wrong?

At practice today, wake up and be aware if you're giving yourself credit.

Practice giving yourself credit for three things you do well today.

DAY 12

YOUR CONFIDENCE IS YOUR RESPONSIBILITY

Let's continue talking about giving yourself credit and gaining gold nuggets.

To put this gold nugget idea to a test, I did a little experiment with my team. I bought a bunch of gold beads at the craft store. I put those beads in a bucket in the locker room, and I called them Confidence Nuggets.

Any time the women worked hard and took a step toward their goal, I told them to take a Confidence Nugget. When the women struggled with feeling like they weren't prepared, I hoped that the gold nuggets could act as proof that they had done enough.

In the beginning of the experiment, I also told the women that they could give Confidence Nuggets to their teammates when they saw them doing something well. I thought it could be great empowerment for our team. What could possibly go wrong with that?

Well, I noticed almost immediately that everyone was handing them away to their teammates, and no one was taking them for themselves. They had no problem seeing what their teammates were doing well, but they weren't giving themselves credit for what they were doing well.

I've learned that women are often happy to celebrate and give credit to others, but they will not do it for themselves.

When I noticed no one was taking the Confidence Nuggets for themselves, I pulled the women in the locker room and I asked them, "Why is everyone handing them away, and no one is taking them for themselves?"

Silence. No one said a word.

I let them know that they didn't have to give me an answer, because I understand how easy it is to see what everyone else is doing well. But I also made the decision to change the rules. They were no longer allowed to give the Confidence Nuggets to their teammates. They had to take them for themselves.

My team started to grumble about the new rule, and my frustration boiled over. I shouted: "Your confidence is YOUR responsibility! It's not anyone else's responsibility to build YOUR confidence!"

They fell silent.

This is where we get into dangerous territory in the sports world. We think that we can get confidence from others. But, please, let this sink in: no one can build your confidence but you.

Others can validate you and say, "Good job," but they can't build your confidence.

As a coach, I learned that I could build up my athletes and tell them how amazing they are, and I could remind them of all the things they've accomplished. They would walk away with their heads held high, feeling confident.

Then they might have a bad practice or competition or get a bad grade on a test or have a fight with their parents or roommate, and everything that I had said to them would be gone.

But when they were giving themselves credit and building their own confidence, no matter what came their way, those Confidence Nuggets didn't go away.

I was working with a client who had been stuck for two years. I learned that she had had a great coach growing up, but he had left two years ago.

As we worked together, we realized that she had given her old coach all the credit for her success. No matter how hard she worked, she believed that the only reason she was good was because of him. She depended on his validation and looked to him to be her Confidence Nugget. When he was gone, her Confidence Nugget was gone, too.

When she started to learn that she was responsible for giving herself credit and building her own confidence, she stopped looking for it from others, and she was able to get unstuck.

Here's the truth: Your confidence is your responsibility.

Do the work:

How did this lesson make you feel?

Could you relate?

Can you see what everyone else is doing well?

Is it hard for you to give yourself credit?

Is it ever good enough?

Do you look at your coach as your Confidence Nugget?

Do you depend on others for validation?

How can you start to validate yourself?

DAY 13

I DESERVE CREDIT

As my team continued with the Confidence Nuggets experiment and the new rule, we ran into a few problems, and those problems taught me so much about women and confidence.

Problem No. 1: If the practice wasn't perfect, they would not take a Confidence Nugget. Ninety-nine things right and one thing wrong, right? After practice, I would ask them if they were going to take their Confidence Nuggets, and they always mentioned the one thing they had done wrong. All the good stuff they had done, all the hard work they had put in didn't matter. They didn't give themselves any credit for it because it wasn't perfect.

Problem No. 2: The women compared like crazy. They would admit, "Yeah, I went fast, but did you see how fast she went?"

"Yeah, that was good, but did you see how good she did?"

Is there an unwritten rule that only one woman can be fast or good at a time?

"If she's fast, I can't be fast."

"If she's good, I can't be good."

Ridiculous! But it's easy to fall into the comparison trap, and that will always lead you to believe that you haven't done enough.

Problem No. 3: If they didn't receive any validation, they wouldn't give themselves credit. If no one said, "good job," it must not have been good enough.

Problem No. 4: I remember a day that a woman came into my office with six Confidence Nuggets. I asked her why she took them.

"I took this one because I beat so-and-so in practice, and she usually beats me," she said.

"I took this one because I did more pull-ups than so-and-so, and she usually does more than me."

She kept going. All six revolved around someone else.

So, I asked her, "Did you know that the day you beat so-and-so in practice, she found out she had failed an important exam right before practice and was in my office bawling her eyes out?"

She scrunched her face and said, "No."

So, I asked her, "What was your effort like in that practice?"

She said, "I about killed myself because I wanted to beat her. I worked my ass off."

THAT is why you take the Confidence Nugget!

"How about on the pull-ups?" I asked.

She said, "I almost popped a blood vessel in my eyeball trying to get that last pull up, so I could beat her."

THAT is why you take the Confidence Nugget!

Now, don't get me wrong, it feels good to beat your teammates and rivals, and it's OK to celebrate those days. But if you rely on building your confidence only when you win, you are going to miss out on so much.

Once the women on my team started giving themselves credit, those Confidence Nuggets were overflowing. This is what it started to look like:

"I worked really hard today, but I caught myself comparing and almost walked out of practice feeling bad about myself. I talked myself through it, found some perspective, and gave myself some credit for my awesome effort, physically and mentally. I'm taking a Confidence Nugget."

"Today, I was not good. My body wouldn't cooperate, and no matter how hard I tried, it just wasn't clicking. But you know what? I kept fighting, and I finished the practice. I'm going to give myself credit for my resilience and take a Confidence Nugget."

"Today in the weight room, I lifted more than I did last week. I'm going to give myself credit for improving and take a Confidence Nugget."

"Today, I walked into practice in a terrible mood. I gave myself a pep talk, got myself into a better place mentally, and had a pretty good practice. I'm going to give myself credit for taking responsibility for my attitude, and I'm taking a Confidence Nugget."

"Today was leg day. I could hardly walk afterward, but I finished. I'm giving myself credit for continuing to fight, and I'm taking a Confidence Nugget."

"There was a party Friday night, but I had practice Saturday morning. Instead of staying out really late, I got home at a decent hour so I could get a good night's sleep. I'm going to give myself credit for making wise decisions and take a Confidence Nugget."

"Today, the dining hall had my favorite cookie! Instead of eating five like I wanted to, I ate one. I'm going to give myself credit for my HUGE sacrifice and take a Confidence Nugget."

As the women gave themselves credit and gained their Confidence Nuggets, I started seeing some of them put one Confidence Nugget on a pin and put it on their backpack. It became their visual reminder of the truth that they had done the work.

Remember the story of Katie Meili on Day 10? I told you that she was able to stay in her truth at the Olympics, which helped her qualify for the finals. She had a little help to keep herself in truth. Before she left, I gave her a bracelet with 10 Confidence Nuggets to represent the 10 reasons why she was going to swim fast. So when the tidal wave of fear came, she could look down at her wrist and be reminded of her truth.

Over the entire Olympic Games, the only time she took off that bracelet was to swim, and she still left it at the top of her swim bag, just to catch a glimpse when she needed help to stay in her truth. Sometimes, all anyone needs is a little reminder.

Here's the truth: You deserve credit, regardless of whether you're perfect, regardless of what anyone else is doing, regardless of if you receive validation, regardless of if you win. When you give yourself credit, regardless, you have proof that you have done the work to be prepared.

Do the work:

How did this lesson make you feel?

Could you relate?

Have you ever not given yourself credit because you weren't perfect?

Because you were comparing?

Because you didn't hear, "good job"?

Because you didn't beat a teammate?

Think about your day. How can you give yourself credit?

DAY 14

COMPARISON TRAP

I've never worked with a client who hasn't failed to give herself the credit she deserves because she was comparing. Comparing is one of the main reasons women feel like they haven't done enough and aren't good enough.

When a woman compares herself to another woman, it is as if that other woman is taking something away from her.

For example, imagine you are going to a social event. You take the time to shower, do your hair and your make up, and you even put on a cute outfit. You look in the mirror, and think, "Wow, I forgot I can be kind of cute."

You leave your house feeling really good about yourself.

But then you get to the event, and it doesn't take you long to notice a drop-dead gorgeous woman across the room.

You start comparing yourself to her, and suddenly, you don't feel so good about yourself. All of a sudden, you don't feel as pretty as you did earlier. Even though you look exactly the same as you did walking out of your door, you're now, somehow, less pretty.

It's as if that woman took your "pretty" away.

Obviously, she didn't, but that's how it feels.

When I explain this story to men, they are dumbfounded. It makes absolutely no sense to them, but I have never met a woman who doesn't know exactly what I'm talking about.

This kind of thinking is like saying, "There can only be one pretty woman at a time. And if it's her, then it can't be me."

Why can't she be pretty, and you be pretty, too?

To make matters worse, anger can creep in. Have you ever been mad at the other woman for taking your "pretty" away? Even though she has done nothing but stand there, you blame her for making you feel bad.

"She is making me feel bad about myself," you might think.

In reality, she's not doing anything. She's not taking anything away from you. You are allowing comparisons to make you feel bad about yourself.

Now, let's take this scenario into your sport.

No matter how well you do, when you compare yourself, it's no longer good enough. And if it's not good enough, you don't deserve credit.

And you wonder why you never feel prepared.

Comparing is one of the biggest killers of confidence. Unfortunately, women seem to do it naturally. I believe that it's been ingrained in most women to compare themselves to others, especially other women.

So, you will never hear me say, "Stop comparing." Because then you will try, you will fail, and then you will beat yourself up, by wondering, "What's wrong with me that I can't stop comparing?"

There's nothing wrong with you.

Instead of telling you to stop comparing, I'm going to tell you to wake up and be aware when you are comparing. (Usually, the best sign that you're comparing is that you feel like garbage about yourself.)

Then pull yourself back to your journey and the steps that you are taking toward your goals. Get your focus back to you. Speak perspective and truth: "Regardless of what anyone else is doing, I deserve credit when I take a step toward my goal."

Here's the truth: When you find yourself comparing, though it may feel like the other woman is taking something away from you, she is not. It is your responsibility to get your focus back to your journey and give yourself the credit that you deserve.

Do the work:

How did this lesson make you feel?

Could you relate?

Do you feel like something is being taken away from you when you are comparing?

Do you find yourself comparing a lot?

Do you feel like you're not good enough when you are comparing?

Do you get mad at other women when you're comparing yourself to them?

How can you get your focus back to your journey?

DAY 15

TAKING YOUR "YAY!" AWAY

Like I said yesterday, I'm never going to tell you to stop comparing. I believe it's become pretty natural for a woman. But I will say this: never allow comparing to take your "yay!" away.

I've seen it way too often. An athlete has a good practice or a good competition, but then they start comparing themselves to others: "She did better. She went faster."

Suddenly, what they did is no longer good enough. Now that "yay!" has gone away, and they walk out feeling like they haven't done enough, and they aren't good enough.

One of my clients had a really good swim meet. She went best times in most of her events and was really happy with her results. Yay!

A week later, though, one of her rivals went to another competition and had a really good meet, too.

When I talked to my client the next week, all she could do was talk about how well her rival did. In her eyes, what she did a week ago was no longer good enough. She felt she deserved no credit for her successful competition, and the fear that she wasn't good enough overwhelmed her.

I finally interrupted her, and I asked her to go through her swim meet and tell me what happened each day. She started on the first day and went through day three, talking about each event and how she felt about it.

When she was done, she said, "Wow! Thank you for making me talk about my competition. I did do well. I had forgotten how well I had done."

That's what comparing does. When she started comparing her meet to her rival's meet, she felt like her rival took away her fast swimming. Of course, she hadn't, but that's how it felt.

Regardless of what her rival did, she deserved to celebrate her "yay!"

But what about when there is no "yay"? When you are stuck in a rut or not performing well, and a rival or a teammate is thriving? How do you not compare in those moments?

Again, there's a good chance that you will find yourself comparing. It's your job to know that you're comparing and pull yourself into some truth and perspective.

Let me forewarn you. The truth and perspective probably won't make you feel a lot better. Let's admit it: no matter how much you like someone, it can be tough to watch people thriving when you're struggling. I get it. And I'm not going to throw a bunch of fluff at you like it's somehow an easy fix.

Everyone's path to success is going to look different. Because someone is getting there before you doesn't mean that your success is not coming. You're on a different path. Just because she has success doesn't mean you're not going to have success. Again, we can all be successful. It's not, "One woman gets success, and the rest of us are out of luck."

And when we keep pulling ourselves back to that truth and perspective, though it may not take away all of your frustration, it does keep you from getting so frustrated that you give up. It will keep you from feeling so bad about yourself that it starts to hinder future competitions.

Here's the truth: When you find yourself comparing, it is your responsibility to pull yourself back to truth and perspective. And it is your responsibility to celebrate your "yay!"

Do the work:

How did this lesson make you feel?

Could you relate?

Do you realize that your "yay!" goes away when you compare?

Have you ever been happy with your performance before you started comparing?

Do you find yourself having a hard time celebrating friends who are thriving?

How can you get yourself back to truth and perspective when comparing?

DAY 16

YOUR BEST IS ENOUGH

I hate to break it to you, but you are not going to be great every day. I have never met an athlete who doesn't have those days when her body won't cooperate, and everything is harder than usual.

But unfortunately, a lot of athletes hold themselves to a perfect standard, and if they are not perfect every day, it's not good enough. And if it's not good enough, they feel like they don't deserve credit.

When I was coaching, I had a young woman on the team who was really consistent. Of course, she wasn't great every day, but she was usually pretty good.

On one particular day, though, we did a test set (a really challenging set that we'd do a few times through the season to measure improvement), and her times were slower than what she usually did. It was one of those days that her body wasn't cooperating, and everything was harder than usual.

Through the entire set, she had to push her uncooperative body through the pain. But she kept fighting. She never gave up, even though it hurt like hell. She cried through the whole thing. I kept thinking, "What a bad ass. So many would have quit by now, but she keeps fighting."

After she finished the set, she got out of the pool and had a breakdown. She yelled, "That was so terrible! What a waste of time!"

A waste of time? Are you kidding me? She just fought and pushed herself through so much pain, but because her times weren't as fast as usual, she was giving herself no credit.

That day, she got better physically. But she didn't get any better mentally. She threw her confidence away.

I shared that story with a former Olympic swimmer, and she told me that she used to beat herself up on those days as well. No matter how hard she worked, if the times weren't fast, she gave herself no credit. She would leave practice mad and beat herself up the rest of the evening.

As she got older, though, she learned to give herself some grace. She realized that she was not going to be great every day. She realized that her best was going to look different on different days.

Some days, going into practice, her best was going to be amazing. Her body would cooperate, things would flow, and she'd be pretty great. But other days, when her body didn't want to move and everything was harder than usual, her best was going to be getting through it and going home.

She made the decision that she was going to put her focus on her effort and give herself credit, even on the rough days. She learned that as long as she was giving her best, she was going to embrace and declare, "It is enough."

It's important to note that this isn't always easy. Your mind will probably want to think, "If it's not great, it's not enough." But you can be like this Olympian and make an intentional decision to choose truth: "My best is always enough."

Because this Olympian embraced this truth, three things happened:

First, she stopped dreading practice.

In the past, she felt she had to be great every day, and she found herself dreading practice because of a What If: "What if I'm not great today?"

When she accepted that her best was going to look different on different days, she could walk into practice knowing that she just had to give that day's best.

Second, she was able to let herself off the hook. She was not going home angry and beating herself up, anymore, because she knew she had given her best.

And third, she gave herself credit on those days that weren't very good.

In the past, no matter how hard she worked, if her times weren't where they were supposed to be, she gave herself no credit.

When she realized that she was not going to be great every day, she put her focus on her effort. She was able to give herself credit when she worked hard, even when the times weren't great.

Here's the truth: Your best is going to look different on different days. But as long as you are giving your best, it is always enough, and you deserve credit.

Do the work:

How did this lesson make you feel?

Could you relate?

Do you find yourself having to be great every day?

Do you dread practices? Why?

Do you beat yourself up after a bad practice?

Do you only give yourself credit when you have a great practice?

How can you start to recognize that your effort deserves a Confidence Nugget?

Helpful hint: A client of mine would set two daily alarms on her phone. As she was walking into practice or a competition, the first alarm was the reminder, "I will do my best." After the practice or competition, she would be reminded with the second alarm: "My best is always enough."

DAY 17

PROCESSING FAILURE

Your best is always enough. But unfortunately, your best will sometimes end up in failure. That is the risk that you take when you do sports. You have to be vulnerable, and you have to risk failure. Those truths keep most people out of sport.

I have seen too many athletes get caught in a rut after a failure. But the failure is not what kept them in the rut. It was their choice to shove the failure down and pretend it wasn't there.

"I don't want to think about it."

"It hurts too bad."

"I'll shove it down and hope it goes away."

But it doesn't just go away.

You must process your failures, or they will become like an anchor in you and keep you stuck.

How do you process failure?

First, face it and feel it. Yep, it hurts. I know you'd rather run from it and avoid failure completely, but you must stop faking it, and face it. As athletes, you are taught that being negative is the worst, so you are always looking for positivity and the silver lining. Give yourself permission to sit in the pain before you go searching for the silver lining.

As you feel it, you're most likely going to go back and forth between sadness and anger. Get it out! Cry, scream, cuss, whatever needs to be done.

But know this, for those who feel more anger than sadness, I heard someone once say that anger is just sad's bodyguard.

Admit it. You're sad. And sometimes the healthiest thing you can do for yourself is get in the shower and cry it out.

After you face it and feel it, ask the hard questions, so you can learn from this failure.

What is my part in this? Take an honest inventory of your life. Sometimes, your first instinct will be to find someone or something to blame. But you must take responsibility for yourself and your career.

Be willing to be brutally honest with yourself and answer:

How's your confidence? Are you really fine, or have you been tap dancing?

How about your nutrition and fueling your body?

How about your work ethic?

Are you getting enough rest and recovery?

What about your priorities? Are they in order?

Remember, the definition of insanity is doing the same thing over and over and expecting a different result. Does anything need to change?

What can I learn from this? Watch the video of your performance, if you have it. Talk to your coaches and support staff about the competition. What could you have done better? How can you be better next time? This is also a great time to take a look back at your training. Does anything need to change?

Is this failure leading me into believing something about myself that isn't true? This one is tough because it takes being brutally honest with yourself. Own it.

What new What Ifs have entered the equation?

We already know one of them will be, "What if this happens again?" Any others?

What truths do I need to remind myself of? Here are some to start with: You experienced a failure, but YOU are not a failure. You are still capable of amazing things. And most importantly, you are still deserving and worthy of success.

Here's the truth: Processing your failures will help you move forward from them.

Do the work:

How did this lesson make you feel?

Could you relate?

Have you ever avoided processing a failure because you just wanted to forget it?

Is there a failure in your past that you need to process?

Go through the steps as if it happened yesterday.

DAY 18

CONFIDENCE JOURNAL

As much as I love the Confidence Nuggets bead idea, some athletes started to run into problems. After a couple weeks, they couldn't remember why they took the Confidence Nugget. Some women didn't care, because they just wanted to see the Confidence Nuggets building up. But some women wanted the specifics of why they were prepared for this moment. They felt more confident when they could see the specific proof.

I started challenging my clients to start a confidence journal. I challenged them to write down at least one thing that they did well in practice every day.

The reason I start with writing only one thing is because most women are so used to focusing on what they are doing wrong that it's sometimes hard to find the good stuff.

When I first started doing one-on-one coaching, I would send my clients 10 Confidence Nuggets and tell them to take one when they were giving themselves credit throughout the week.

No one came back with all 10 Confidence Nuggets. Not one person could find 10 things they could give themselves credit for during the week. They usually came back with five or six, even though,I could watch one of their practices and probably see 10 things they did well.

So, the goal is one. And as you search for the one, your brain is going to start finding more good stuff. Suddenly, you will start filling the page with tons of credit.

After you've written in your journal consistently, it will serve as proof that you have done the work and that you are prepared. Reading its pages that tell of all the hard work, dedication, and sacrifice, is going to remind you that you are a bad ass.

The journal is so important for three reasons:

1. It's a good reminder.

As I mentioned earlier, Katie Meili used to write down 10 reasons why she was going to swim fast. A lot of clients have taken that idea and tweaked it. They write down three to five reasons why they deserve to perform well. They feel like 10 reasons are hard to remember, especially when they are feeling the pressure. And they like knowing that they deserve to perform well.

I was speaking to a client one day as she was writing her reasons. She said, "I work hard. I don't know what else to put down."

Five minutes before she said that, she was flipping through her confidence journal, saying, "Oh, this day was so insane! It was so hard, and I worked my ass off." She told me about so many workouts that she called "insane."

So, I asked, "What was so insane? Those are the reasons why you deserve to perform well. Find the specifics and focus in on the insanity that you put yourself through in practice. Those are going to be the reminders that you're a bad ass."

2. It's motivating. I had a client who was really talented, but she could be lazy sometimes. Being so good so young, she never learned how to push herself past pain. When she started writing in her confidence journal, she found motivation to keep pushing in

practice because she wanted to be able to go home and write in the journal. She found accountability and motivation by keeping the journal.

3. It's proof of your strength. Sometimes, you can uncover more confidence from off days than good days. Documenting a day when your body wouldn't cooperate and nothing seemed to go right, but you gave your best and didn't give up, can be the proof you need that no matter how you feel at a competition, you always find a way to show up and fight.

Here's the truth: A confidence journal can be your proof that you are a bad ass.

Do the work:

How did this lesson make you feel?

Could you relate?

I challenge you to start a confidence journal. Every day, write down at least one thing that you are doing well. Before competitions, go through it and be reminded of all your hard work that has prepared you for this moment.

DAY 19

RUFFLE FEATHERS

Your confidence journal is going to be a great reminder of your truth. And hopefully, it will help you get comfortable in that truth.

Today, I want to challenge you to start speaking your truth.

Did you know that in the business world, one of the biggest frustrations among employers is that women won't sell themselves in interviews? They are reluctant to talk about their strengths or accomplishments. They don't want to be seen as arrogant or sound like they're bragging.

Even when they could bring so much value and expertise, many women will shrink back and water down their truth, which leads to missing out on great opportunities.

Just like we saw in the team building exercise from Day 7, many women are uncomfortable in their truth, especially saying it out loud.

When I ask you to talk about your gifts, I want you to be comfortable speaking about them. And when I ask you if you agree, I want you to boldly say, "Yes, of course, I do. I know my truth."

I have seen that when women get comfortable in their truth and they are not afraid to speak their truth, they are the most powerful. Because, again, confidence always revolves around truth.

I was talking about this subject with a client, and she asked me, "Can we speak our truth without ruffling feathers?"

I was quick to answer, "Nope. Confident women usually ruffle feathers."

At the 2019 FIFA Women's World Cup, the U.S. National Team was victorious. It seemed like the entire country was finally paying attention to a woman's sport, in this case, soccer. It was amazing! When the players got home, New York City threw a parade for the women. They were so happy, cheering and celebrating.

One particular moment caught my eye. It was player Megan Rapinoe, holding the trophy. She was holding it in front of her, admiring it, and the camera caught her saying, "I deserve this. I deserve this."

I'll admit my first reaction was, "She's so cocky." It was my natural response. But then I called myself out, and asked, "Why is this cocky? Does she not deserve the trophy?"

Of course she does! She has given her life to her sport. She has worked her ass off for years, given millions of hours, and sacrificed to be the best. The truth is, she deserves that trophy, and she is allowed to speak her truth.

I was so inspired by her being comfortable in her truth, I decided to put the video on my social media. I wanted to promote a woman speaking her truth!

Well, sadly, it didn't go well. I ended up turning off the comments on the post because I couldn't stand to see another person ripping her to pieces: "She's so cocky. She's so arrogant. Ever heard of humility? She's so full of herself."

It was deflating. But I get it. My first reaction was the same. It's what we've been taught.

And then I thought, *can you imagine the reaction if this were a man enjoying his trophy, saying he deserves it?* It's easy to imagine people thinking, *Wow, I wish I could be confident like him! I couldn't love him more!*

I read the nasty comments; they were from both men and women. Unconscious gender bias has led both men and women to believe that women should shrink back and water down their truth. It's something that we desperately need to unlearn.

Megan Rapinoe ruffled some feathers that day. I can't help but giggle when I think if she cared what other people had to say. She knows she deserves the good stuff that comes from her hard work. She embraces her truth and speaks it—just like men get to do every day. She went home a champion, regardless of what others thought of her.

I want to challenge you to speak your truth, but I also want to challenge you to check your reaction when other women speak theirs. Your first reaction may be ugly, just like my initial reaction to Megan saying she deserved the trophy.

But then, remember the truth: Women deserve all the good stuff that comes from their hard work. Women are allowed to be proud of themselves. Women are allowed to talk about their accomplishments. Women are allowed to celebrate their victories. Women are allowed to speak their truth.

Your reaction may lead a woman to either shrink back and shut up or step forward and continue to embrace and speak her truth. Let's encourage speaking truth!

You will ruffle some feathers with your confidence, but that's OK. Embrace your truth. Speak your truth. And encourage other women to speak theirs.

Here's the truth:

You are not being arrogant when you talk about your accomplishments. You are not bragging when you talk about your gifts and what you're great at. You are not being cocky when you speak your truth.

Do the work:

How did this lesson make you feel?

Could you relate?

Does this lesson make you really uncomfortable?

Do you think you can start speaking your truth?

Challenge yourself to get uncomfortable and speak your truth boldly.

How do you react when other women speak their truth?

Can you call yourself out if your initial reaction is to think she's being cocky?

Challenge yourself to encourage other women to speak their truth.

DAY 20

KNOW YOURSELF AND TRUST YOURSELF

For the last 10 days of this book, you will dive deep into finding consistent confidence. Consistent confidence comes when you know yourself well and you are making consistent decisions that are best for you. You find consistent confidence when you get really good at taking care of you.

A teenage swimmer client of mine, who was struggling with fear and anxiety before her races, told me that she had been told to visualize her races. I asked her what that looked like. She said that she would visualize her race and see herself racing the other swimmers. And then she would see herself win.

I mentioned that seeing myself win would probably add more fear and pressure to me, but if it works for her, great!

About 15 minutes later, she said, "Christen, I can't stop thinking about what you said. I think seeing myself win the race is adding fear and pressure for me, too! I think that's why I'm feeling so anxious before my races."

We learned that she was the one adding more fear and pressure onto herself when she visualized herself winning.

I asked her why she was visualizing that way, and she told me that she had met a really good triathlete who did it and told her to do it, too. She took the triathlete's advice and didn't even question whether it would work for her.

As she thought about what really works for her, she realized that she does like to visualize. But she changed her tactics to visualize herself with no one else in the pool. This allowed her to ease the anxiety before her races.

This young woman took advice, but she didn't pay attention to how it affected her. She was standing behind the blocks completely anxious, and yet she kept doing the visualization because in her mind, if it worked for this great athlete, then it must work for her, too. She was completely unaware that this way of visualizing wasn't working for her.

To know yourself, you have to wake up and be self-aware. You need to pay attention to what works for you and what doesn't.

Life is a journey of realizing things about yourself. But you only realize things when you're paying attention. And you must have the courage to be brutally honest with yourself because not everything that you realize is pretty.

Wake up and get to know yourself:

How are you wired? How does your mind work?

What works best for your body?

What brings you joy?

What depletes you?

What makes you sad?

What motivates you?

When do you feel like your best self?

When do you feel like your worst self?

When do you feel really confident?

When do you feel really insecure?

What triggers you?

What are your weaknesses?

What are your strengths?

As you become self-aware and get to know yourself, you will start to trust that you know what will work and what won't work for you. You get really good at taking care of you.

Here's the truth: When you know yourself and trust yourself, you can take care of yourself well and make decisions that work best for you.

Do the work:

How did this lesson make you feel?

Could you relate?

Do you feel like you know yourself well?

Are you willing to be brutally honest with yourself?

Do you trust yourself?

When you get advice, do you think about whether it will work for you?

Do you trust that you know what you need? Why or why not?

DAY 21

SELF-CARE

Yesterday, we talked about finding consistent confidence when you know yourself well and you get really good at taking care of you.

Today, let's talk about self-care.

The definition of self-care that I appreciate the most is this: the practice of taking an active role in protecting one's own well-being and happiness.

When you know yourself well, you know what's good for your well-being and happiness. And you also know what isn't. You are able to make consistent decisions that are best for you.

When I was coaching, I learned to give my athletes mental health days. I understood that the grind of sport is real. It's easy for life to feel like a constant rotation of eating, sleeping, school or work, and sport. It can deplete you physically and mentally.

If my athletes needed a practice off to take care of themselves, all they had to do was send me a text saying, "mental health day." They didn't need to tell me why. They didn't need to give me any details. I trusted that they knew themselves better than anyone, and if they needed a practice off, I encouraged it.

Some would use it to take a nap. Others would catch up on schoolwork or maybe get a massage. I knew doing these things would be so much more helpful than coming to another practice and getting even more depleted. Because when you get depleted, confidence is hard to come by.

The next day at practice, I saw that they could breathe easier. A weight had been lifted. They made a decision that was best for them. They protected their well-being, their happiness, and their confidence

Through the years, I have encouraged my athletes to get to know themselves and learn what works best for them for self-care.

Self-care activities run the gamut: taking walks, reading books, driving with the windows down blasting music, laughing, taking a day off from the phone, a bath and face mask, sitting outside and enjoying nature, lying in bed watching murder mysteries, getting a massage, creating art, talking to a therapist, and much more.

Everyone is different and unique. What works for your teammates and friends may not work for you. Find what works best for you.

Another form of self-care is asking for help.

If you are struggling with nutrition, ask for some help. If you are struggling in school, ask for help. If you are struggling with your mental health, ask for help.

Finding a counselor to talk to is one of the best decisions I've ever made, and I do absolutely consider counseling or therapy to be self-care.

Remember, it's OK to not be OK. But it's not OK to do nothing about it. Speak your truth. Have the courage to be honest with yourself, and if you need to find a counselor or therapist, talk to a parent, a friend, a coach or staff member, or do some research on your own. Take care of you and make that call.

It's important to know that your first therapist or counselor who you work with may not be the best fit for you. That's OK! Don't give up! Make another call and find a better fit. I promise you, it's worth it.

Take care of you.

Here's the truth: Taking care of you and practicing self-care is a necessary piece of finding consistent confidence.

Do the work:

How did this lesson make you feel?

Could you relate?

How do you protect yourself from the grind?

How do you protect your well-being and happiness?

What do you do for self-care?

Do you ever feel guilty for taking time for yourself? Why?

Do you need to ask for help?

Who can help you?

DAY 22

HEAL

Making the choice to heal is part of self-care.

As a college coach, I always joked that I spent most athletes' freshmen years helping them heal from the junk that parents and coaches put them through.

The pushing, the prodding, the mental abuse, the expectations, the pressure—it was like living in a jail. When these athletes had freedom in college, many realized how dysfunctional it all was.

One of my athletes had had a lot of success when she was young, so she moved away from her parents to an "academy" where she went to school and trained.

Because she was so good, Coach paid a lot of attention to her and he was kind to her. But then she started growing, she hit a slump, and she got stuck. Coach no longer wanted anything to do with her, and his kindness was long gone. After that, she never got any better. She continued to stay stuck for years.

She was so angry and disappointed in her experience with this coach, and she was so relieved to go to college and leave this coach behind. She was desperate for a fresh start.

She came into school like Kelsi—excited, determined, and ready to work hard. But unfortunately, her freshman year, nothing was really changing. She continued to stay stuck. So I started talking with her, hoping we could figure out how to get her unstuck.

In one of our conversations, she brought up her old coach. She mentioned that he was not nice to her, but whenever I would ask questions, she'd say she didn't really want to talk about it. "It's over, he was an ass, I've moved on," she would say.

But I could tell she hadn't moved on. So I kept meeting with her, and the more we got to know each other, the more she trusted me. The more she trusted me, the more she was willing to share what really happened with her coach.

She shared the stuff he would say to her, and my jaw was on the ground. Not only had his kindness gone away, but he went out of his way to be awful to her. It was very clear that he had beaten the confidence out of her. No wonder she'd been stuck all these years.

I asked her how she would handle those awful comments, and she said that she just tried to numb herself because she never wanted to react to him. She didn't want to give him the satisfaction of knowing that he hurt her feelings or made her cry.

But he *did* hurt her feelings. Just because she didn't face it didn't mean the pain wasn't there.

Seeing my response made her realize how toxic her environment had been, and she started to feel the need to talk about it. Once she started to talk, the dam broke. It all came out, as well as all the tears that had been stored up for years because she didn't want him to see her cry.

For years, she took her pain and shoved it down, numbed herself and thought that by ignoring it, it would go away. But as you've learned, it doesn't just go away. It became like an anchor and kept her stuck.

By facing him, his words, and her pain, she was able to get rid of the anchor and get unstuck. And the best part? She felt freedom from him, too. He no longer had power over her. His hurtful words had been living in her heart for so long, that when she faced them, he was gone, too. She was free.

I've seen this sort of experience over and over again.

A professional athlete that I was working with had had a really bad college experience. Her coaches were verbally abusive toward her. When she reached out to me to start working together, she already knew that this is what she was going to have to face.

She shared her story with tears running down her face. It was clear that the pain was still living in her. In the beginning of her freshmen year, she had fought their bad behavior. She spoke up about it, but that caused them to fight back. Their relationship became pretty volatile. Slowly, she learned to just stay quiet and shrink back while they did their best to avoid her.

I asked her why she never transferred to another school, and she had a very familiar response. She didn't want to give them the satisfaction. Leaving, she felt, would show them that she wasn't strong enough to take it. But by staying, she continued in a toxic environment. And toxic environments always cause damage.

I first had her write letters to the coaches who had hurt her. She wasn't going to send them, but I wanted her to get some power back and say what she'd been wanting to say for so long.

As she read the letters out loud to me, we realized that being in that toxic environment for so long had led her to believe that she wasn't worth her coaches' attention and wasn't good enough. She was walking through life and her professional career with thoughts of "I'm not worthy" leading the way.

When she finally faced the truth, she was able to see that it was the coaches and the toxic environment that caused her to believe these lies. When she realized why she believed those lies, she also realized they weren't true. What a breakthrough. She was free.

I hope that not everyone reading today's lesson can relate. But I have heard so many stories similar to these over the years that I feel it's important to address abuse and healing in these 30 days.

Healing is self-care. When you find the courage to face your pain and heal, you can break free from the pain, the person, and the lies that they created in you. I like to remember the words of author and speaker Iyanla Vanzant: "If you don't address the wounds of the past, you continue to bleed."

Here's the truth: Healing can free you to move forward toward your fullest potential and greatest confidence.

Do the work:

How did this lesson make you feel?

Could you relate?

I know today goes pretty deep. I hope you're willing to go deep if you need to. The pain you may be holding onto doesn't have to come from coaches. I want you to think about any wounds that need to be healed.

What do you need to face?

Do you need to break free from some pain?

Do you need to write some letters?

Are you believing any lies because of someone's behavior toward you?

DAY 23

FINDING BALANCE

Ever been on the verge of a breakdown? I bet that some of you have. I'd also guess it's because you held your feelings and emotions in for too long, or you're sick of the sport-eat-sleep grind.

Breakdowns can be ugly. Ever scare yourself when you finally snap? I know you probably laugh, because you know exactly what I'm talking about. It's common to reach a breaking point and feel like you've got nothing left to give, except anger, tears, and frustration.

Do you feel confident when you're on the verge of a breakdown? I can answer that for you. I've had too many calls with women having a breakdown, and they feel like they can find no stability, no control, and certainly no confidence.

Let's talk about the importance of speaking consistently.

I used to offer the women on my team an hour a week or every two weeks when they could come into my office and get things off their chest. They could speak about everything going on in sport and in life. Some of the meetings were 15 minutes and were just a check in, but sometimes they took the entire hour with lots of crying and Kleenex.

All the women on my team took me up on this hour, except one. She said that she was fine and didn't need to meet with me. I respected her decision.

But she was in my office every five to six weeks, having a major breakdown, bawling her eyes out and feeling like she had no stability or control.

She held it all in, and it took that long for it to be too heavy. Then, she would blow.

She'd get it out, leave my office and then let it build up for another five to six weeks. The cycle continued, and she consistently struggled with finding stability and confidence.

Had she talked it out consistently, she could have avoided the breakdowns, and she could have found balance and consistent confidence.

Another athlete really struggled with finding balance in her life. But it wasn't because she wasn't speaking consistently.

One day she came into my office, grabbed the Kleenex and said, "All I do is go to school, swim, sleep, and eat. That's my whole life. School, swim, sleep, eat."

Sound familiar?

It's easy to get caught in a dangerous cycle of only focusing on one or two priorities in your life, while the rest get put on the back burner.

One day, I asked her when she'd last been out and had some fun. She gave me a confused look, wondering why her coach would be asking that, and she said, "It's been a few weeks. On the weekends, I'm usually catching up on schoolwork or sleeping."

I challenged her to have some fun on Saturday night. I told her to put her books down by 7 p.m., get in the shower, get cute, find a great outfit, and go out and have some fun!

I reminded her that fun did not mean getting trashed and staying out until 6 a.m. I think we can all agree those nights don't lead into us being our best. I told her to get out and be social. Take her mind off of the school, swim, sleep, and eat grind.

She looked at me like I was crazy and said, "You're the only coach in the world who would encourage her athletes to go out." Maybe. But I'd learned the importance of balance.

When she came into practice on Monday, I could see that a weight had been lifted. She actually thanked me for telling her to go out. She had gotten dinner with friends, and it was a nice change from the usual grind. She felt stable, balanced, and back in control.

I think sometimes we fear making huge changes to our schedules, but finding a healthy balance is not usually huge changes. It's small ones. It's just doing something to pull yourself out of the everyday grind.

I worked with an Olympian who had no life outside of sport. Her whole world revolved around sport. If she had a bad practice or a bad competition, it was like the world was ending. She would go home and think about it non-stop and beat herself up over it.

She knew this wasn't working, and she had to make some changes. She needed to give herself some grace and understand that her best was going to look different on different days. She also desperately needed to find some balance in her life.

I asked her what she liked to do outside of sport, and she had a hard time figuring it out. She looked back at her childhood and said that she used to enjoy doing puzzles. So I challenged her to start doing puzzles when she got home from practice. She had forgotten how much she enjoyed doing them, and it actually helped. She was able to put her focus on the puzzle instead of sport all the time.

Feeling the difference that little change made, she started doing more things that she enjoyed and ended up getting a weekend retail job. It didn't take any time away from her sport, but it did give her some balance, and it gave her people outside of her sport to talk to as well.

Suddenly, her entire life didn't revolve around sport, and if she had a bad practice or competition, she was able to move forward from it much more easily. All of this added up to her performing at an even higher level.

A professional athlete client of mine was struggling with finding balance outside of sport, and she really needed a hobby. She discovered canvas weaving, and she fell in love with it. It brought her balance, but it also brought out her creativity. She felt alive! It connected her with others who enjoyed it as well, and it opened up a new world that was so exciting and different than the world of her sport.

Having found stability and balance, she's performing better in her sport than she ever has, and she even started a small business selling her pieces.

These women knew themselves well enough to know that something had to change. They did not want their world to only revolve around sport. They knew they had to find some balance in their lives. Those decisions brought joy, stability, and consistent confidence.

Here's the truth: Finding balance helps you find consistent stability, which always leads to consistent confidence.

Do the work:

How did this lesson make you feel?

Could you relate?

Do you need to find some balance in your life?

Do you need to speak more consistently?

Who can you talk to?

What are your hobbies? What do you enjoy doing?

What are some things you can do to find balance and stability?

DAY 24

YOUR INNER CIRCLE

A vital piece of finding balance is choosing the right people to be in your inner circle. Your inner circle is the small circle of friends that you keep closest to you. Whom you choose to allow into that circle is one of the most important decisions of your life.

Ever heard of the saying, "Show me your friends, and I'll show you your future?" As a college coach, I saw that play out consistently. The people whom you choose to spend your time with are some of the biggest influencers in your life, your career, your environment, and your future.

I want to start this discussion with an overview of romantic relationships. I was a college coach for a long time, and I've seen healthy relationships that bring joy into my athletes' lives. But I've also seen a lot of unhealthy relationships, and I've never seen anything take down a woman's confidence faster than a toxic romantic relationship.

Let's go straight to truth.

Love is not unkind. It doesn't physically hurt you. It doesn't emotionally hurt you. It doesn't call you names.

Love is not feeling like you have to always prove that you're worth their time, their effort, their love.

Love is not crying yourself to sleep because you feel unloved and ignored.

Love is not waiting for unanswered texts and phone calls.

Love is not walking on eggshells to ensure you always say the right thing.

Love is not feeling uncomfortable in revealing the real you. Your real personality. Your imperfect body. Your flaws. Your past.

Love is not unfaithful. It's not losing little pieces of your soul as you have sleepless nights worrying what they're doing and who they're with.

Love is not tearing you down.

Love is not ignoring you.

Love is not deceitful and a bunch of excuses.

Love is not being too busy and treating you like you are not a priority.

Love is not making you feel ordinary.

When you allow people into your life who don't value you, you'll inevitably start feeling that you're not valuable. When you're always heartbroken, it's easy to begin to feel weak. When you have to work so hard to get attention, it's easy to feel that you're not that special. When you're never a priority, it's easy to feel that you're not worth it and you're not enough.

Confidence can't live there.

If you find yourself in a toxic relationship, speak truth. Tell a parent, friend, or coach. You are not alone, and you don't have to walk this journey alone.

And remember, you deserve amazing, but it's your responsibility to choose amazing.

The same goes for your friendships. You deserve amazing friendships, but it is your job to choose the right people.

Your time and your space are sacred. Be very careful about whom you allow into that space.

Your inner circle of friends must be trustworthy. You will always know that they have your back, no matter what. You will feel comfortable speaking your truth.

They have great character. They are genuinely good people with extraordinary hearts that will fiercely love you.

They are ambitious. They have big dreams and don't want to settle into mediocrity, either. Together, you will inspire each other.

They support. They will walk with you every step of this journey, and when you need to lean on them, they are there.

They encourage. When you are struggling, they will be there to inspire you to keep moving forward.

They offer wise advice. They think things through and always think of your best interest.

They have the courage to speak truth to you. We all need a good kick in the ass, sometimes. Your inner circle of friends should have the courage to speak truth, even when it's not what you want to hear.

Your inner circle may change in different seasons of your life, and there may be seasons that your inner circle is empty. I'd rather it be empty than filled with the wrong people. In every season, it is your responsibility to choose wisely.

Remember, your space is sacred. Protect it.

Here's the truth: Your inner circle will be the biggest influencers in your life. You deserve amazing relationships, but it's your responsibility to choose amazing.

Do the work:

How did this lesson make you feel?

Could you relate?

Who is in your inner circle?

Is there anyone whom you need to step back from?

Is there anyone you don't fully trust?

Are you in a romantic relationship?

Is it healthy?

Do you need to start speaking truth about your relationships?

DAY 25

BOUNDARIES

Choosing your inner circle is a really important decision. But obviously, there are other people in your life as well. Some of those people aren't always healthy for you to be around, and they aren't good for your well-being and happiness.

Creating boundaries around people in your life can be really hard, but it is an essential part of self-care. It's an essential part of finding consistent confidence.

Boundaries will change as you go through life.

In high school, you may need to create boundaries around mean girls at your school or on your team.

Unfortunately, mean girls are often the popular girls. It's easy to want to be part of that group. Many teenage clients of mine have tried to reach out to the popular girls, but they've been rejected or just completely ignored.

Creating boundaries with these girls is as easy as changing your perspective. As we talked about yesterday, your space is sacred, and you should not allow unkind or unfriendly people into your sacred space. When you create boundaries to keep mean people out of your space, suddenly those girls are not "rejecting" you. Instead, you are committing an act of self-care.

In college, you may need to create boundaries around friends or teammates who party too much, stay out too late, or bring drama into your life.

These people don't live the same lifestyle as you. They don't have the same priorities as you. They probably don't have the same goals as you.

You must protect your well-being and happiness and create some boundaries with them, especially during your competitive season. It's OK to pull back and spend less time with them. If you're really close with them, you might want to let them know that you are creating these boundaries. That can be hard, but your responsibility is to protect yourself. Their reaction to your boundaries is not your responsibility.

As an adult, you might need to create boundaries around your family members.

When I work with professional athletes, I often hear things like, "Every time my family calls, they just want to talk about Olympic Trials. I feel so much pressure. I don't want to talk about it all the time."

One client of mine had a family member who bought a ticket to the Olympic Games before she even qualified. That was added pressure that she did not need!

Another client has a sibling who is really negative and always says something bad about her appearance and weight. It's exhausting every time she's with her.

Yes, you are allowed to create boundaries around your family members. You are allowed to tell them what you are willing to talk about with them. And you are allowed to let them know that if they cross your boundaries, you will be taking a step back.

Because again, it is your responsibility to protect your well-being and happiness.

Creating boundaries is an act of self-care.

Here's the truth: Creating boundaries protects your confidence, well-being, and happiness.

Do the work:

How did this lesson make you feel?

Could you relate?

Who, in your life, needs some boundaries?

What can you do to protect yourself?

What can you say to them?

Think about how you can create boundaries around people you have to see everyday.

DAY 26

SOCIAL MEDIA BOUNDARIES

Social media can be such a fun world, but it can also be a dangerous place. It can deeply affect your confidence, your well-being, and your happiness.

I hear things like:

"I was so excited because I did 12 pull-ups! That's more than I've ever done! I was feeling so strong, but then I started scrolling and saw an athlete posted a video of herself doing 20 pull-ups. Now, 12 sucks, and it's no longer good enough."

"I'm so proud of how hard I've been working lately. And I'm proud I've found a workout schedule that works best for me and my body. Then I started scrolling and saw an athlete working out and she looks so athletic. Now, I fear I'm not doing enough."

"I've been so proud of myself with my nutrition. I've made it a priority, and I'm making wise decisions. I feel fit and strong. Then I started scrolling, and I saw one of my rivals in a bikini, and she has a six-pack. Now, I'm finding everything wrong with my body, and I don't feel strong or fit anymore."

"All I do is train, and all my friends are posting pictures of how much fun they're having. My life sucks."

Social media is one big comparison trap. I've watched it derail some of the best athletes in the world. Too many times, I've seen someone finally making progress and feeling good, but then they get on social media, and they start to feel bad about themselves. Their "yay!" completely goes away.

I want you to start thinking about creating boundaries and limiting time on social media as self-care. Boundaries are a great way to take an active role in protecting your well-being, happiness, and confidence.

You know yourself. You know what's best for you. You know what triggers you. You know what makes you feel bad about yourself.

It may be time to do a social media cleanse and mute or delete the accounts that lead you down a rabbit hole of comparing and feeling bad.

And yes, some of those accounts might belong to your friends. You don't have to delete, but at least mute them. Remember, it is your responsibility to protect your well-being. Sometimes, that means making uncomfortable decisions.

A lot of clients of mine delete their social media completely a couple of weeks before a big competition. They know where comparing leads them, and they are taking responsibility to protect their well-being and confidence. It has made a huge difference in their lives. I highly recommend it.

It's also important to remember that a lot of social media is filled with pictures and posts that aren't even real.

A few years ago, I was talking to a woman who was having problems with her husband. They had stopped communicating, and her resentment was building. She shared that a couple of nights previous, her anger had boiled over, and she threw a remote control at him. Luckily, it missed, but because she threw it so hard, it put a hole in the wall.

A few weeks later, she had posted on social media photos from a family photo shoot. The pictures were beautiful. They looked like the happiest family on Earth. All the comments were about how lucky she is to have such an amazing, happy family.

You have no idea what's really going on in someone's life. Social media is not going to show you the whole truth. Just like you don't share the lowlights, no one else does, either.

Take care of you. Create boundaries with your social media to protect your well-being, happiness, and confidence.

Here's the truth: Social media can be a comparison trap. Protect yourself by creating boundaries.

Do the work:

How did this lesson make you feel?

Could you relate?

Is it time to do a social media cleanse?

What pics really throw you into comparing?

What accounts lead you into feeling bad about yourself?

What do you need to delete?

Any friends that you need to mute?

Think about your habits around social media. Are there long-term changes you need to make?

DAY 27

BODY CONFIDENCE

Your relationship with your body can be complex, and it is very personal. Today, I want to keep it simple and share three important lessons that I've learned from my coaching career:

1. I will never tell you to buy into the idea of body positivity and loving your body, because for a lot of you, that will lead to your faking it. You know that confidence always revolves around truth, so you don't have to say that you love your body, if you don't love your body.

But I have learned that you don't have to love your body to have a healthy relationship with your body. I do believe that you can learn to accept your body.

Body acceptance is the concept that you don't have to love your body, but you can accept it. On Day 4, we talked about being real and positive. I believe body acceptance is all about being real and positive.

You can be real, and you don't have to fake a love that you don't have for your body. But this is your reality today. This is your body today. So instead of hating on your body, declare: This is me. I will accept my body and get my focus back on how to be my best and give my best in this moment.

2. Finding body neutrality helps you put your focus on what your body can do, as opposed to what it looks like. This allows you to find some gratitude for what your body can do for you.

I was working with an Olympian who had put on some weight. She seemed to think about her body all the time, and she put herself down daily. She had grown up in a home where her mom and sister hated their bodies and talked about them incessantly, so it was natural for this athlete to hate her body, too. And now with the extra weight, the hate grew.

She was so happy to realize that she didn't have to reach "body positivity." She was allowed to be real. But she made a pact with herself. She knew that she wasn't going to say anything good about her body, but she committed to not saying anything negative about her body, either. She stayed neutral.

Whenever she found herself ripping her body to pieces, she stopped herself and pulled herself back to her commitment. She then put her focus on what her body was going to do for her that day. And when she thought about all that her body was going to do for her, she was able to find perspective and gratitude. She found gratitude in the truth that her body allows her to do what she loves to do.

3. If you are struggling with an eating disorder or disordered eating, it is time to speak truth. Eating disorders and disordered eating thrive in secrecy and hiding, and we've already learned that confidence can't live there.

Please know that you are not alone. Just like fear, everyone thinks they're the only one struggling, so no one talks about it. Remember, it's OK to not be OK, but it's not OK to do nothing about it. Speak your truth to a trusted person. Talk to a parent, friend, coaches, or staff about getting help.

Be aware, the person who you tell may not fully understand. When I first started coaching, a young woman shared her truth with me, and I told her to just stop doing what she was doing. I had no idea how to handle that situation. Thankfully, she gave me another chance, and we were able to get her some help. She was no longer alone or hiding, and it changed her life forever.

In the 20 years since that moment, I have walked with so many women on their journeys of speaking truth, getting help, and learning how to have a healthy relationship with food and their bodies. It is worth it. You are worth it.

Speak truth. You are not alone. You are worthy of a healthy relationship with your body.

Here's the truth: You don't have to love your body to have a healthy relationship with your body.

Do the work:

How did this lesson make you feel?

Could you relate?

Do you struggle with your relationship with your body?

How can you improve your relationship with your body?

How can you find gratitude for your body?

Do you think you need to find some help?

Whom can you talk to about getting help?

DAY 28

I CHOOSE ME

When I ask female former athletes what their greatest regrets are from their career, I often hear, "I wish I'd been more selfish."

When I ask them to explain, I hear that they wish they had not worried so much about what everyone else thought and that they had done what was best for them.

Remember the story of the Confidence Nuggets? When I first started the experiment with my team, I told them that they could give the Confidence Nuggets away to their teammates as well. But then I noticed the women were not taking them for themselves. I changed the rules because their confidence is their responsibility.

After that meeting when I changed the rules, a young woman came up to me and said, "I think I know why no one is taking the Confidence Nuggets for themselves."

I was surprised to hear her say, "It's kind of embarrassing."

I'm sorry, what? It's embarrassing to give yourself credit for making the choice to work hard and take steps toward your goals?

But I listened. And she said, "What if I take a Confidence Nugget for myself, and one of my teammates sees me and kinda rolls her eyes wondering, 'Does she really think she worked hard today?'"

I said, "Let me get this straight. The same woman that you're handing a Confidence Nugget to because you can see the good stuff she's doing is the same woman you're afraid is going to roll her eyes and judge you when you take one for yourself?"

She looked confused but thought about it and said, "I guess that sounds crazy, but yep!"

These women would rather throw away their chance to build confidence than have someone possibly roll their eyes and judge them.

Because they worried so much about what everyone else thought, they did not do what was best for them.

As a college coach, I always had an array of personalities on my team. And every year, after a few months of school, at least one of them would come to my office and cry, telling me how miserable she was.

One year, the crying, miserable girl came into my office and didn't want to leave. So we sat and chatted for a while. As she told me about her life outside of the pool, she described herself as "kinda nerdy." She loved to read, she liked school and learning new things, and she thrived on being low-key with no drama.

But she explained that no one else on the team really enjoyed doing the things she liked to do. They all wanted to party, meet boys, and socialize. That wasn't really her scene, but she was desperate to fit in, so she had been going out with her teammates on the weekends and partying. She didn't like partying, and she didn't like drinking, but to fit in, she joined them every weekend. In her mind, at least she wasn't the "loser" alone in her dorm, reading a book.

She was faking it to fit in. As usual, she just figured if she faked it, she'd somehow make it. But she was miserable, and she felt as if she had no confidence.

I challenged her to spend the next weekend doing what she loved to do. She was nervous about telling her teammates that she wasn't going out, but she did it.

I saw an immediate difference in her. She felt so good staying true to herself that she was like a different woman. She even carried herself differently.

After that first weekend of choosing what was best for her, it became easier and easier for her to make that choice. Teammates even sometimes joined her. But if she had to be alone, she chose to stay true to herself. Not only did it do good for her soul, but she was proud of herself. Being proud of yourself always leads to confidence.

Here's the truth: Staying true to yourself will lead to feeling confident that you are doing what's best for you.

Do the work:

How did this lesson make you feel?

Could you relate?

Do you find yourself worrying about what others think?

Are you staying true to yourself?

Are there things you need to change in your life?

Declare it: "I choose me, even if I have to stand alone."

DAY 29

LOVE YOURSELF, REGARDLESS

We talk to ourselves more than anyone else in the world. What are you saying to yourself?

Are you harder on yourself than anyone else? Do you hold yourself to a perfect standard, while giving grace and love to others? Would you ever say to your friends or loved ones what you say to yourself?

I was speaking to an Olympian who had a lot of success as a teenager. She won Olympic medals, and life was grand. But then she hit a slump, and sport and life went downhill fast. She feared that all of her fans and people who loved her would turn their backs on her because she wasn't performing well.

So I asked her what she felt she needed to do to be loved. She spent the week thinking about it and came back with a list.

Her list said:

I need to perform well.

I need to be pretty.

I need to be fit and skinny.

I need to get good grades.

I need to say the right things.

I need to dress the right way.

I need to have it all together.

I need to be happy and positive all the time.

She had tears in her eyes as she said her list out loud.

I then asked her, "If you could write yourself a permission slip for anything, what would that permission slip be?"

She thought about it and said that she needs a lot of them, but if she were to choose just one, it would be, "I will love myself, regardless."

Regardless of any of those things on her list, she was going to make the choice to love herself. Regardless of what anyone else thought, she would love herself.

Can you imagine a world where women would love themselves, regardless of the lists they have for themselves?

Can you imagine a life where you would love yourself, regardless?

Here's the truth: To find real confidence, you need to like yourself. You need to be proud of yourself. You need to love yourself, regardless.

Do the work:

How did that lesson make you feel?

Could you relate?

What's on your list?

What permission slips do you need to write to yourself?

How can you find a way to love yourself, regardless?

DAY 30

CONFIDENCE IS A COMMITMENT

You made it! You're confident for life!

Just kidding.

Real confidence is a lifelong journey. What you've learned these last 30 days is going to be your roadmap.

I'm proud of you for finishing this month of study, but it's very important to know that finishing doesn't mean you're going to be confident forever and you'll have no worries. Confidence is a daily decision. Sometimes, it's a minute-by-minute decision.

Confidence is a commitment. Commit yourself to these actions:

I will stay awake and aware of my thoughts.

I will speak openly about my What Ifs, fears, and doubts.

I will stop faking it, get real, and own it.

I will be real and positive.

I will stop having temper tantrums and accept that I cannot predict the future.

I will lean into the vulnerability of being all in.

I will focus on truth that I believe down deep.

I will embrace my truth and be comfortable in it.

I will take responsibility that I am thinking something at all times.

I will activate the angel and speak perspective and truth to panic.

I will choose truth.

I will give myself credit.

I will embrace that my confidence is my responsibility.

I will pull myself into perspective when I'm comparing.

I will not allow comparing to take my "yay!" away.

I will remember that my best is always enough.

I will process my failures and learn from them.

I will keep a confidence journal for reminders of my truth.

I will ruffle some feathers and speak my truth.

I will encourage other women to speak their truth.

I will get to know myself well.

I will protect my well-being and practice self-care.

I will heal.

I will find balance in my life.

I will be wise about whom I allow into my inner circle.

I will create boundaries around people in my life.

I will create boundaries around social media.

I will create a healthy relationship with my body.

I will choose me.

I will love myself, regardless.

I will continue to do the work.

Here's the truth:

You are ready. You are prepared. You know what to do. You got this!

Do the work:

Continue to journal.

Continue to speak your truth.

Continue to do the work.

ABOUT THE AUTHOR

Christen Shefchunas is a professional confidence coach who works with athletes ranging from Olympians, world champions and NCAA All Americans to high school athletes. As a former Division I head coach, Christen watched too many young women miss out on their potential because of their lack of confidence. Realizing that there was a significant lack of resources for these athletes, Christen left her 16-year coaching career and started Coach Christen, a business focused on helping female athletes. She works one-on-one as a confidence coach with some of the best female athletes in the world, and she speaks to teams, athletes, women's organizations, and women in business about confidence, handling fears, and what to do in those "pressure-to-perform" moments. She is the creator of Confidence Nuggets, a bracelet line created to remind women of their truth.

Learn more at: coachchristen.com

9 781735 919331